GOVERNMENT PROCEDURES AND OPERATION

SOCIAL AND BEHAVIORAL SCIENCE USED IN THE ADVANCEMENT OF POLICY

APPLICATIONS AND INSIGHTS

GOVERNMENT PROCEDURES AND OPERATION

Additional books in this series can be found on Nova's website under the Series tab.

Additional e-books in this series can be found on Nova's website under the e-book tab.

GOVERNMENT PROCEDURES AND OPERATION

SOCIAL AND BEHAVIORAL SCIENCE USED IN THE ADVANCEMENT OF POLICY

APPLICATIONS AND INSIGHTS

ERIKA STEPHANS
EDITOR

nova publishers
New York

Library of Congress Cataloging-in-Publication Data

ISBN: 978-1-63484-293-8

Published by Nova Science Publishers, Inc. † New York

CONTENTS

Preface		**vii**
Chapter 1	Social and Behavioral Sciences Team Annual Report *Subcommittee on the Social and Behavioral Sciences Team*	**1**
Chapter 2	The Power of Prompts: Using Behavioral Insights to Encourage People to Participate *Nadine Dechausay, Caitlin Anzelone and Leigh Reardon*	**75**
Index		**123**

PREFACE

The Federal Government administers a wide array of programs on behalf of the American people: financial aid to assist with college attendance, social insurance programs and tax incentives to promote retirement security, health insurance programs to ensure access to healthcare and financial protection for families, disclosure requirements to help people obtain safer mortgages, and others. But Americans are best served by these programs only if the programs are easy to participate in and present options and information clearly. When programs are designed without these considerations in mind, Americans can incur costs that go beyond lost time and frustration. Research from behavioral science demonstrates that seemingly small barriers to engagement—such as hard-to- understand information, burdensome applications, or poorly presented choices—can prevent programs from working effectively for the very people they are intended to serve. In 2014, the White House Office of Science and Technology Policy (OSTP) established the Social and Behavioral Sciences Team (SBST) to ensure that our best understanding of behavior—how people engage with, participate in, and respond to policies and programs—is integrated into the policymaking process. This book examines the social and behavioral sciences used in the advancement of policy.

In: Social and Behavioral Science … ISBN: 978-1-63484-293-8
Editor: Erika Stephans

Chapter 1

SOCIAL AND BEHAVIORAL SCIENCES TEAM ANNUAL REPORT*

Subcommittee on the Social and Behavioral Sciences Team

EXECUTIVE OFFICE OF THE PRESIDENT
NATIONAL SCIENCE AND TECHNOLOGY COUNCIL

Dear Colleagues:

The Obama Administration has made significant progress both in using and building evidence to improve government performance and deliver better results at a lower cost for the Nation. A strong body of evidence demonstrates that research insights about behavior, when incorporated into the design of Federal programs and policies, have significantly improved Americans' lives, whether by boosting retirement savings nationwide or helping more low-income students get to college each year.

Building on this work, in 2014, the White House Office of Science and Technology Policy assembled the Social and Behavioral Sciences Team (SBST)—a cross-agency group of experts in applied behavioral science that translates findings and methods from the social and behavioral sciences into

* This is an edited, reformatted and augmented version of a report issued by the Office of Science and Technology Policy, of the National Science and Technology Council, September 2015.

improvements in Federal policies and programs. The Social and Behavioral Sciences Team Annual Report represents SBST's successful efforts in its first year to apply behavioral insights to Federal policy and to measure the impact of these applications on key policy outcomes using rigorous evaluations.

The report covers two core areas on which SBST focused in its first year: streamlining access to programs and improving government efficiency. As a result of SBST projects, more Service-members are saving for retirement, more students are going to college and better managing their student loans, more Veterans are taking advantage of education and career counseling benefits, more small farms are gaining access to credit, and more families are securing health insurance coverage. And improvements in government program integrity and efficiency are saving taxpayer dollars.

The publication of this report marks an important milestone for the Administration's policy of using behavioral insights to strengthen the ways in which Federal programs and policies serve the Nation—a policy that was codified in September 2015 by an Executive Order entitled "Using Behavioral Science Insights to Better Serve the American People." This Executive Order directs agencies to: (i) identify policies, programs, and operations for which behavioral insights may yield substantial improvements in social welfare and program outcomes; (ii) develop strategies for implementing these insights and rigorously testing and evaluating their impacts; (iii) recruit behavioral science experts to join the Federal Government; and (iv) seek opportunities to strengthen agency relationships with the research community to better utilize findings from the social and behavioral sciences.

I look forward to seeing further results from the Team's efforts to leverage behavioral insights to improve outcomes for the Nation. I am confident that the results in this report represent a solid foundation on which to build future work.

Sincerely,
John P. Holdren
Assistant to the President for Science and Technology
Director, Office of Science and Technology Policy

EXECUTIVE SUMMARY

The Federal Government administers a wide array of programs on behalf of the American people: financial aid to assist with college attendance, social insurance programs and tax incentives to promote retirement security, health insurance programs to ensure access to healthcare and financial protection for families, disclosure requirements to help people obtain safer mortgages, and others.

But Americans are best served by these programs only if the programs are easy to participate in and present options and information clearly. When programs are designed without these considerations in mind, Americans can incur costs that go beyond lost time and frustration. Research from behavioral science demonstrates that seemingly small barriers to engagement—such as hardto-understand information, burdensome applications, or poorly presented choices—can prevent programs from working effectively for the very people they are intended to serve.[1]

For example, one behavioral science study found that a complex application process for financial aid was more than just a hassle: it discouraged applications for aid, and actually led some students to delay or forgo going to college altogether.[2] Fortunately, behavioral science not only identifies aspects of programs that can act as barriers to engagement, but also provides policymakers with insight into how those barriers can be removed. That same study showed that streamlining the process of applying for financial aid—by providing families with application assistance and enabling families to automatically fill parts of the application form using information from their tax return—increased the rates of both aid applications and college enrollment.

When *behavioral insights*—research findings from behavioral economics and psychology about how people make decisions and act on them—are brought into policy, the returns are significant. Because the Federal Government leveraged insights from the financial aid study and simplified the process of applying for Federal student aid, college is now more readily accessible to millions of American families.[3] Similarly, the Pension Protection Act of 2006, which codified the practice of automatically enrolling workers into retirement savings plans, is based on behavioral economics research showing that switching from an opt-in to an opt-out enrollment system dramatically increases participation rates.[4] Since the implementation of this policy, automatic enrollment and automatic escalation have led to billions of dollars in additional savings by Americans.[5]

In 2014, the White House Office of Science and Technology Policy (OSTP) established the Social and Behavioral Sciences Team (SBST) to ensure that our best understanding of behavior—how people engage with, participate in, and respond to policies and programs—is integrated into the policymaking process. SBST is a cross-agency group of experts in applied behavioral science that translates findings and methods from the social and behavioral sciences into improvements in Federal policies and programs for the benefit of the American people. SBST works to identify how behavioral insights can be integrated into Federal agency programs in order to help agencies achieve their missions and objectives.

As detailed in this report, SBST efforts are already paying dividends for Americans. Due to SBST projects, more Servicemembers are saving for retirement, more students are going to college and better managing their student loans, more Veterans are taking advantage of education and career counseling benefits, more small farms are gaining access to credit, and more families are securing health insurance coverage. And improvements in government program integrity and efficiency are saving taxpayer dollars.

Results from SBST's First Year

Over its first year, SBST focused on executing proof-ofconcept projects where behavioral insights could be embedded directly into programs at a low cost and lead to immediate, quantifiable improvements in program outcomes. To generate reliable evidence about the effectiveness of integrating behavioral insights into programs, SBST designed these projects, in nearly all cases, as randomized trials. This report presents the results of all completed SBST projects, including projects that did not yield statistically significant improvements.

Because SBST projects are designed to address only the behavioral barriers that affect how people engage with programs, project effects can be modest. Yet, because behavioral changes to program administration often require little or no additional cost, returns on investment can be large even when project effects are small. It is no more expensive to send an effective version of an email than an ineffective one.

In building an initial portfolio of work, SBST focused on projects in two areas where behavioral science had a strong role to play and impacts could be demonstrated relatively rapidly: (1) streamlining access to programs and (2) improving government efficiency.

Streamlining Access to Programs

Working closely with agencies across the Federal Government, SBST used behavioral insights to expand program reach and promote retirement security, increase college access, connect workers and small businesses with economic opportunities, and improve health outcomes.

Promoting Retirement Security

- To promote participation in the Thrift Savings Plan (TSP), a workplace savings plan for Federal employees, SBST and the Department of Defense (DOD) launched an email campaign that sent approximately 720,000 unenrolled Servicemembers one of nine email variants, designed using behavioral insights, notifying recipients of the opportunity to participate in TSP. Compared to no message, the **most effective message nearly doubled the rate at which Servicemembers signed up** for TSP. Emails informed by behavioral insights led to roughly **4,930 new enrollments and $1.3 million in savings in just the first month** after the emails were sent. DOD is now scaling up this intervention by sending periodic emails informed by behavioral insights to Servicemembers about the benefits of TSP.
- To further promote saving, SBST and DOD prompted Servicemembers to make a "Yes" or "No" choice about whether or not to contribute to TSP during an orientation briefing upon their arrival at a new military base. **More Servicemembers enrolled in TSP during the prompted choice pilot: 8.7 percent of non-enrolled Servicemembers, compared to 2.9 percent on average at three comparison bases, and 4.3 percent during comparison time periods at the pilot base.** Based on the success of this pilot, DOD is committing to applying insights from this pilot across bases and installations with higher troop concentrations.
- To assist nearly 140,000 Servicemembers who were required to re-enroll in their Roth TSP in order to continue making contributions, SBST and DOD redesigned an email that alerted Servicemembers of the requirement to re-enroll. The redesigned email **led 22 percent more Servicemembers to re-enroll in TSP within a week**— 3,770 more re-enrollments than among those sent a standard message. Based on this result, DOD immediately scaled up the successful messaging in subsequent outreach reminding Servicemembers to re-enroll in TSP.

Improving College Access and Affordability

- To help students enroll in college, SBST and the Department of Education's (ED) office of Federal Student Aid (FSA) provided technical expertise to researchers and the nonprofit uAspire on messages notifying college-accepted, high school graduates of required pre-matriculation tasks for their respective colleges. A series of eight personalized text messages to low-income students reminding them to complete these tasks **led to a 5.7 percentage point increase in college enrollment**, from 66.4 to 72.1 percent.
- To help Federal student loan borrowers stay on top of their payments, SBST and FSA sent a reminder email to over 100,000 borrowers who had missed their first payments. The reminder email **led to a 29.6 percent increase in the fraction of borrowers making a payment** in the first week after it was sent, from 2.7 to 3.5 percent.
- To increase awareness of income-driven repayment (IDR) plans among student loan borrowers, SBST and FSA sent an informational email about IDR plans to over 800,000 borrowers who had fallen behind on their payments. The low-cost, timely message led to a **fourfold increase in applications for income-driven repayment plans**, with 4,327 applications for IDR made within twenty days of the email being sent.

Advancing Economic Opportunity

- To increase Veterans' uptake of education and career counseling benefits, SBST and the Department of Veterans Affairs (VA) sent notices informing Veterans of their benefits and the steps needed to apply. Relative to simply notifying them of their eligibility, **highlighting to Veterans that they had earned the benefits led nearly 9 percent more Veterans to access the application for those benefits.** This increase represents only 146 additional Veterans clicking through to the application form, however, suggesting that barriers to accessing this program lie elsewhere.
- To improve economic outcomes for small-scale and specialized farmers, SBST and the United States Department of Agriculture (USDA) collaborated on a campaign to increase knowledge and utilization of loan options. **Farms that were sent a personalized letter with a customized set of action steps for applying for a Microloan were 22 percent more likely to obtain a loan**, representing an increase from 0.09 to 0.11 percent.

Helping Families Get Coverage and Stay Healthy

- To assist individuals and families with obtaining health insurance, SBST and the Department of Health and Human Services (HHS) sent one of eight behaviorally designed letter variants to each of more than 700,000 individuals who had already begun the enrollment process, but had not yet completed an application. **Those sent the most effective version of the letter were 13.2 percent more likely to enroll in health insurance** than those sent no letter, with enrollment rates of 4.56 and 4.03 percent, respectively.

Improving Government Efficiency

Many measures of government efficiency depend on the decisions and actions of individuals such as program officials, beneficiaries, and contractors. SBST applied behavioral insights to improve program integrity, save money on operational expenses, and identify programs the Government could run more efficiently.

Promoting Program Integrity and Compliance

- To improve the accuracy of sales figures self-reported by vendors selling goods and services to the Government, SBST and the General Services Administration (GSA) redesigned an online data-entry form to include a signature box at the top of the page in which the user had to confirm the accuracy of self-reported sales. Because vendors pay to the Government a small fee based on those sales reports, introducing this box led to **an additional $1.59 million in fees collected within a single quarter**. Based on this result, GSA is making permanent changes to the form to incorporate a signature box.
- To increase debt recovery from individuals with outstanding non-tax debt, SBST worked with the Department of the Treasury's Debt Management Service (DMS) to redesign a collection letter. **No difference in payment rates** was observed, but changes such as shortening the web address for making an online payment **led 45 percent more individuals to pay online**, representing an increase from 1.5 to 2.2 percent. DMS has now permanently shortened the web link in the collection letter.
- To reduce inappropriate prescribing of controlled substances, SBST and HHS's Centers for Medicare and Medicaid Services (CMS) sent

providers with unusually high billing patterns a letter comparing their prescribing rates with the prescribing rates of their peers, as well as educational information about proper prescribing practi ces. **No measurable impact was seen on prescription rates.**

Ensuring Cost-Effective Program Operations

- To determine if letters could encourage security holders to transfer accounts to an online platform, SBST collaborated with the Department of the Treasury's Bureau of the Fiscal Service to design outreach to account holders. Letters that included a personal appointment time with a call center led to **23 percent higher call-in rates** than standard letters, representing an increase from 10.6 to 13.0 percent. Account conversion rates remained low for both groups, however. Based in part on this result there are no further mailings planned.
- To increase response rates to a workplace survey that determines Federal office space management strategies, SBST and the GSA worked together to incorporate behavioral insights into the timing and messaging of emails announcing the survey. Among other findings, **email click rates were highest at lunchtime**, with 15.3 percent of emails sent at 11:55 a.m. resulting in recipients clicking through to the survey, compared with 13.3 percent at 8:55 a.m.
- To encourage double-sided printing, SBST and the USDA's Economic Research Service (ERS) created a dialog box that asked employees to change their default printer setting to double-sided after employees had initi ated a single-sided print job. This **prompt increased the likelihood of double-sided printing by 5.8 percentage points**, from a baseline of 46 percent. Based on this fi nding, ERS plans to change the default setting of all printers to double-sided.

SBST's initial portfolio of work has led to real improvements in outcomes that matter for Americans and demonstrated that Federal agencies can successfully integrate behavioral insights into their programs. The results of SBST projects completed to date represent a foundation on which the Federal Government, can, moving forward, base decisions about both program administration and policy design. Based on results from SBST pilots, agencies have already made lasting reforms to program administration in order to better serve the American people.

I. Introduction

> "A growing body of evidence demonstrates that behavioral science insights—research findings from fields such as behavioral economics and psychology about how people make decisions and act on them—can be used to design government policies to better serve the American people...By improving the effectiveness and efficiency of Government, behavioral science insights can support a range of national priorities, including helping workers to find better jobs; enabling Americans to lead longer, healthier lives; improving access to educational opportunities and support for success in school; and accelerating the transition to a low carbon economy."
>
> **— Barack Obama, Executive Order entitled "Using Behavioral Science Insights to Better Serve the American People"**

The Federal Government administers a wide array of programs on behalf of the American people: financial aid to assist with college attendance, social insurance programs and tax incentives to promote retirement security, health insurance programs to ensure access to healthcare and financial protection for families, disclosure requirements to help people obtain safer mortgages, and others.

But Americans are best served by these programs only if the programs are easy to participate in and present options and information clearly. When programs are designed without these considerations in mind, Americans can incur costs that go beyond lost time and frustration. Research from behavioral science demonstrates that seemingly small barriers to engagement—such as hard-to-understand information, burdensome applications, or poorly presented choices—can prevent programs from working effectively for the very people they are intended to serve.[1]

Consider, as an example, financial aid for college. One behavioral science study found that a complex application process for financial aid was more than just a hassle: it discouraged applications for aid, and actually led some students to delay or forgo going to college altogether.[2] Fortunately, behavioral science not only identifies aspects of programs that can act as barriers to engagement, but also provides policymakers with insight into how those barriers can be removed. That same study showed that streamlining the process of applying for financial aid—by providing families with application assistance and enabling families to automatically fill parts of the application form using information from their tax return—increased the rates of both aid applications and college enrollment.

When *behavioral insights*—research findings from behavioral economics and psychology about how people make decisions and act on them—are brought into policy, the returns are significant. Because the Federal Government leveraged insights from the financial aid study and simplified the process of applying for Federal student aid, college is now more readily accessible to millions of American families.[3] Similarly, the Pension Protection Act of 2006, which codified the practice of automatically enrolling workers into retirement savings plans, is based on behavioral economics research showing that switching from an opt-in to an opt-out enrollment system dramatically increases participation rates.[4] Since the implementation of this policy, automatic enrollment and automatic escalation have led to billions of dollars in additional savings by Americans.[5]

Social and Behavioral Sciences Team

An effective and efficient government must reflect our best understanding of behavior—how people engage with, participate in, and respond to policies and programs. But scientific advances do not translate into policy improvements without a coordinated effort. Policy design and program administration must actively integrate behavioral science research findings, and promising findings must be adapted to a government context.

To meet this need, in 2014 the White House Office of Science and Technology Policy (OSTP) established the Social and Behavioral Sciences Team (SBST). SBST is a cross-agency group of experts in applied behavioral science that translates findings and methods from the social and behavioral sciences into improvements in Federal policies and programs for the benefit of the American people. SBST works to identify how behavioral insights can be integrated into Federal agency programs in order to help agencies achieve their missions and objectives.

SBST is chaired by OSTP and has representation from a dozen member agencies across the Federal Government, as well as offices within the Executive Office of the President (EOP). SBST also receives critical support from the General Services Administration's (GSA) Office of Evaluation Sciences (OES), which recruits behavioral science experts from within and outside of government to work on SBST efforts.

As detailed in this report, SBST efforts are already paying dividends for Americans. Due to SBST projects, more Servicemembers are saving for retirement, more students are going to college and better managing their student loans, more Veterans are taking advantage of education and career counseling benefits, more small farms are gaining access to credit, and more families are securing health insurance coverage. And improvements in government program integrity and efficiency are saving taxpayer dollars.

Building on SBST's successful first year, on September 15, 2015, President Obama signed an Executive Order entitled "Using Behavioral Science Insights to Better Serve the American People."

Executive Order: Using Behavioral Science Insights to Better Serve the American People

The Executive Order formally establishes SBST and directs Federal agencies to integrate behavioral insights into their policies and programs. Specifically, the Order directs agencies to: (i) identify policies, programs, and operations where applying behavioral science insights may yield substantial improvements in public welfare, program outcomes, and program cost effectiveness; (ii) develop strategies for applying behavioral science insights to programs and, where possible, rigorously test and evaluate the impact of these insights; (iii) recruit behavioral science experts to join the Federal Government; and (iv) strengthen agency relationships with the research community to better use empirical findings from the behavioral sciences.

To implement this directive, this Executive Order charges SBST with providing policy guidance and advice to help agencies achieve these objectives. Pursuant to the Executive Order, SBST focuses on four areas where prior research and practice indicate that behavioral insights play an especially strong role in program outcomes: [6]

- SBST looks for opportunities to help qualifying individuals, families, and businesses access programs and benefits by streamlining processes that may otherwise limit participation.
- SBST works to improve how the government presents information to consumers, borrowers, and program beneficiaries, by giving greater consideration to ways in which information format, timing, and medium can affect understanding.
- Where programs and policies offer choices, SBST works to carefully consider how the presentation and structure of those choices, including default settings and the number and arrangement of options

can empower participants to make the best choices for themselves and their families.

- Where policies create incentives to take specific actions, such as saving for retirement, SBST considers how the frequency, presentation, and labeling of benefits, taxes, subsidies, and other incentives can more effectively and efficiently promote those actions, with a particular focus on opportunities to use nonfinancial incentives.

SBST works with agencies to develop specific recommendations for modifying elements of program design or administration, based on findings from behavioral science research.[7] Close collaboration with these agencies facilitates adaptation of these insights to the specific context of each program.

For further discussion of how SBST works with agencies to identify promising applications of behavioral insights, see "Identifying Federal Applications of Behavioral Insights."

Identifying Federal Applications of Behavioral Insights

Applying behavioral insights in the right context can lead to substantial improvements in program outcomes. Given the vast array of policies and programs across the Federal Government, and the full range of their objectives, how does SBST identify where to apply behavioral insights? SBST has found that three key elements define the most promising opportunities to apply behavioral insights:

Policy Goals: SBST projects support well-defined policy goals or already-identified program challenges—for example, improving program integrity in Medicare to save taxpayer dollars. Successful projects require clear goals in part because SBST itself does not set policy.

Individual Behavior: SBST projects identify a link between a policy goal or program outcome and the decisions or actions of individuals.

This link is the essence of an SBST project. When Federal policy outcomes do not depend on behavior, applications of behavioral insights will have little relevance, no matter how worthwhile the goal.

Program Touchpoints: SBST projects operate at a point of direct interaction between the Federal Government and individuals. This point could be an application process or form, a website that offers program choices, publicly available information about government resources, or the structure of incentives (both financial and nonfinancial). SBST explores how behavioral insights can inform that interaction in ways that can potentially improve outcomes. If the goal is to help borrowers manage their student debt, for example, the application process for alternative repayment plans represents a touchpoint where behavioral insights could help borrowers choose the option that is right for them.

Results from SBST's First Year

The report that follows presents results from all fully completed SBST projects. In building an initial portfolio of work to apply behavioral insights to improve program and policy outcomes, SBST drew on lessons from many sources—academic research, precedents at the Federal level, and beyond.[8] In particular, SBST builds on the efforts of pioneering agencies, such as the Department of Health and Human Services (HHS), the Department of Agriculture (USDA), and the Department of Labor (DOL), which are already using behavioral insights to assist low-income families, promote healthy food choices, and design better labor market policies.[9]

Over its first year, SBST focused on executing proof-of-concept projects in two areas where behavioral insights could be embedded directly into programs at a low cost and where quantifiable improvements in program outcomes could be demonstrated relatively rapidly:

1) **Streamlining access to programs:** Projects to streamline access to programs in retirement security, education, economic opportunity, and health care.
2) **Improving government efficiency:** Projects to improve program integrity, promote efficiency among Federal employees, and help officials make cost-effective decisions.

To generate reliable evidence about the effectiveness of integrating behavioral insights into programs, SBST designed these projects, in nearly all cases, as randomized trials (details about the methods used on each project are given in the project abstracts collected below, "Appendix: SBST Project Abstracts"). Randomized trials are considered the gold standard of evidence among policymakers and social scientists because they allow for robust causal inference— the estimated impact can be said to be due to the implemented change, rather than other factors. And because these methods identify both what works and what does not, SBST reports the results of all of its completed projects, including projects that did not yield statistically significant improvements.[10]

For additional discussion on the role of evidence in SBST's application of behavioral insights, see "Behavioral Insights and the Role of Evidence."

As the results detailed in this report show, SBST projects have led to real improvements in outcomes that matter for Americans, and have demonstrated that Federal agencies can successfully integrate behavioral insights into their programs. Because these projects are designed to address only the behavioral barriers that affect how people engage with programs, project effects can be modest. For example, there are many reasons why people may choose not to enroll in a retirement savings program. A behavioral insights project that sends an email notice about the program might make a difference for someone who had been intending to enroll, but just needed a reminder. But it would not be expected to make a difference for someone who hadn't enrolled because, say, he or she was focused instead on saving for other goals, like a down payment on a house. Yet, because behavioral changes to program administration often require little or no additional cost, returns on investment can be large even when project effects are small. It is no more expensive to send an effective version of an email than an ineffective one.

The results of SBST projects completed to date represent a foundation on which the Federal Government, can, moving forward, base decisions about both program administration and policy design. Agencies have already made substantive reforms to program administration based on results from SBST pilots.

The results in this report contribute to establishing a compelling evidence base for why, how, and where Federal policymakers should consider further applications of behavioral insights to program design.

Behavioral Insights and the Role of Evidence

At its core, SBST's role is one of translation: from academic research findings to pragmatic program solutions. But designing the best way to communicate with the public, to structure choices and incentives, and to help qualifying individuals access public programs, is not as simple as conducting a review of the scientific literature. Decades of behavioral research reveals that how individuals respond to the presentation of information or the structure of choices, for example, is highly context specific.[1]

As a result, this process of translation requires constant evaluation and feedback. SBST works with agencies to, where possible, rigorously test the impact of these insights on program outcomes before implementing them widely. In this way, SBST can learn about what works, what works best, and what does not work. To achieve this goal, SBST often implements randomized trials. Randomized trials are considered the gold standard of evidence among policymakers and social scientists because they allow for robust causal inference: the estimated impact can be said to be due to the implemented change, rather than any other factors.

This type of evaluation often is worthwhile because the effects of these projects can be meaningful and the costs of the evaluation can be low. Behavioral science indicates that small details of program administration— the timing of a mailing or the order of choices presented on a website—can matter more for program outcomes than might be expected.[2] Randomized trials that test the impact of behavioral insights such as these can often be embedded directly into the administration of a program at little cost, and impacts can be observed at little cost using existing administrative data. Even when impacts are modest, they can return savings or benefits that far outweigh the expense of either the intervention or the evaluation.

[1]Daniel Kahneman and Amos Tversky, "Prospect Theory: An Analysis of Decision Under Risk," *Econometrica* 47 (1979): 263–291. Amos Tversky and Itamar Simonson, "Context-Dependent Preferences," *Management Science* 39 (1993): 1179–1189.

[2]Richard H. Thaler and Cass R. Sunstein, *Nudge* (Yale, 2008).

II. Streamlining Access to Programs

People can realize the benefits of Federal Government policies and programs only if they can access them. Behavioral science research demonstrates that seemingly small barriers to engagement, such as hard-to-understand information, burdensome applications, or poorly presented choices, can prevent programs from effectively reaching the very people they are intended to serve.[11]

SBST used behavioral insights to streamline access to programs that promote retirement security, increase college access, connect workers and small businesses with economic opportunities, and improve health outcomes.

a. Promoting Retirement Security

Retiring with financial security is a widely shared goal among workers. Federal policies support this goal by encouraging private savings, protecting workplace pensions, and providing Social Security retirement benefits. Behavioral insights such as automatic enrollment, where the default setting is for workers to be enrolled in a workplace savings plan and action is required on the part of workers only if they choose not to participate, have already helped millions of workers in the private sector save for their retirement. The civilian workforce of the Federal Government has benefited as well; since 2010, civilian agencies have automatically enrolled new hires in a defined contribution plan, the Thrift Savings Plan (TSP).

Unlike their civilian counterparts, Servicemembers are not automatically enrolled by the Federal Government in TSP. While 87 percent of civilian Federal employees are enrolled in TSP, just 42 percent of active duty Servicemembers are enrolled. To make TSP more accessible for interested Servicemembers, SBST worked with the Department of Defense (DOD) on a series of pilots informed by behavioral insights that encouraged participation in TSP and prevented already-enrolled Servicemembers from losing access to TSP benefits.

Enrollment in Thrift Savings Plans

To help Servicemembers interested in saving for the future participate in TSP, SBST and DOD launched an email campaign notifying non-enrolled Servicemembers of the opportunity to sign up for TSP, the potential benefits of investing, and the steps required to enroll.[12] Research demonstrates that timely, clear messages of this kind can help individuals better understand their options, make more informed decisions, and follow through on their intentions.[13] Prior to this pilot, DOD did not routinely send targeted communications about TSP to non-enrolled Servicemembers.

Together with DOD, SBST designed eight email variants with different combinations of features based on behavioral insights. These features included: providing clear steps to enrollment, framing the decision to enroll as a choice between two options ("Yes, I want to enroll" or "No, I do not want to enroll"), displaying projected financial returns to investing in TSP, and making salient either the short- or long-term benefits of participating in TSP.[14] SBST also designed a ninth email variant with language drawn from the TSP website.

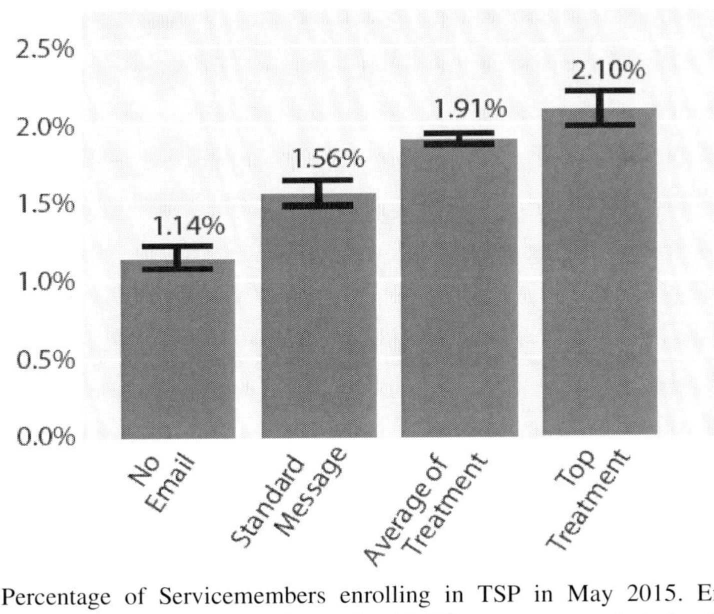

Notes: Percentage of Servicemembers enrolling in TSP in May 2015. Error bars display 95 percent confidence intervals. Al differences are statisticaly significant at the 5 percent level. n = 806,861.

Figure 1. Servicemember TSP Sign-Up Rates in May 2015.

In late April 2015, each of the 806,861 Servicemembers not enrolled in TSP was sent either the TSP website language email, one of the eight email variants designed using behavioral insights, or no email (the business-as-usual practice).

Emails significantly increased Servicemember enrollment in TSP. Figure 1 shows the fraction of each group that signed up for TSP in May 2015. Servicemembers who were sent the emails that incorporated behavioral insights had an average enrollment rate that was 0.77 percentage point higher than those who had not been sent an email. A portion of this effect—0.42 percentage point—is due to simply sending an email, while the remaining effect is a result of incorporating behavioral insights into the content of the email.

The increase in enrollments due to the emails informed by behavioral insights, relative to no email, translates into 4,930 additional TSP enrollments and $1.3 million in additional savings by Servicemembers in a single month. The most effective email, which clarified the action steps needed to enroll in TSP and emphasized the potential long-term benefits of saving even a little each month, nearly doubled the rate at which Servicemembers signed up for TSP.

Based on the success of this pilot, DOD committed at the 2015 White House Conference on Aging to apply these insights at scale by sending periodic emails informed by behavioral insights to Servicemembers about the benefits of participating in TSP.[15]

Prompting a Choice for Thrift Savings Plans

Building on the outreach effort detailed above, SBST and DOD developed a second pilot to further increase Servicemember participation in TSP. Behavioral science research indicates that prompting individuals to make a decision about whether or not to take an action at a relevant point in time can help motivate action among those who are interested.[16] For example, asking employees to actively choose whether or not to participate in workplace savings plans has effectively increased enrollment in these plans.[17]

Based on this insight, SBST and DOD implemented a project that prompted a choice regarding whether or not to enroll in TSP at an orientation session for Servicemembers who were moving to a new military base. For Servicemembers, the point at which they move to a new base—a transition often tied to changes in compensation and duties—is a natural moment to offer such prompts. SBST designed a cover sheet that featured a box to check indicating a "Yes" or "No" decision about enrolling in TSP (as shown in Figure 2), as well as general information about TSP and the benefits of investing. The cover sheet was circulated, along with the TSP application form, to Servicemembers at an orientation session at a military base during the pilot period.

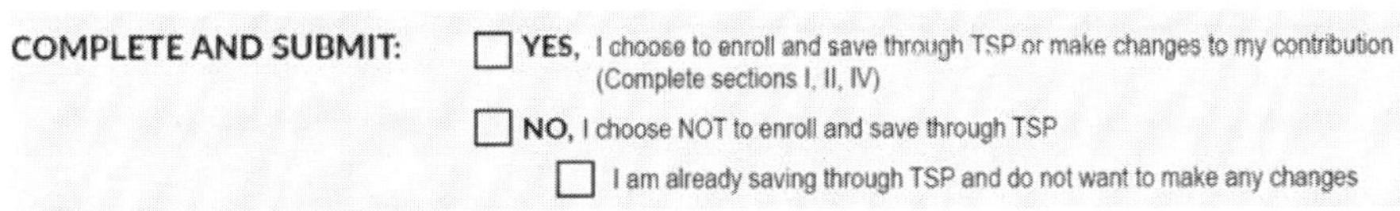
COMPLETE AND SUBMIT: ☐ YES, I choose to enroll and save through TSP or make changes to my contribution (Complete sections I, II, IV)
☐ NO, I choose NOT to enroll and save through TSP
☐ I am already saving through TSP and do not want to make any changes

Notes: As part of a prompted choice pilot, Servicemembers were presented with the check-box above as part of other paperwork they were already required to complete during in-processing.

Figure 2. TSP Prompted Choice.

As shown in Figure 3, introducing a prompted choice resulted in substantially higher TSP enrollment rates among Servicemembers. Enrollment rates were initially similar at the pilot base and three comparison bases (4.34 and an average of 2.88 percent, respectively), but the prompted choice generated a much higher rate at the pilot base (8.71 percent), compared to average rates at the three comparison bases over the same period (2.91 percent on average). Taking into account differences across both the time periods and the different bases, the prompted choice intervention is estimated to have led to a 4.3 percentage point increase in the rate at which non-enrolled Servicemembers enrolled in TSP.

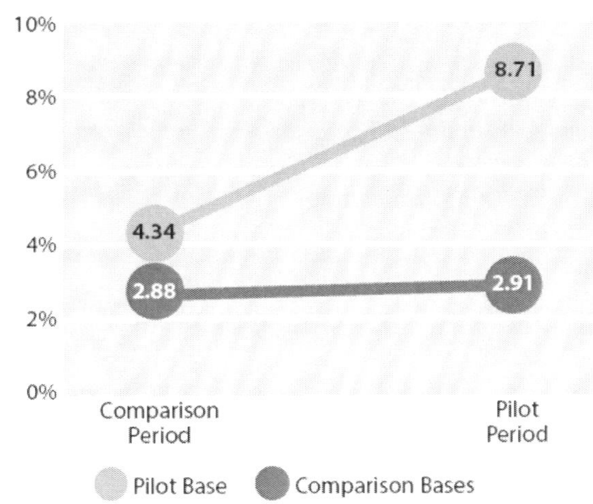

Notes: Enrolment rates for TSP among non-enroled, in-processing Servicemembers at the pilot base and comparison bases during the pilot period and the earlier, comparison period.

Figure 3. Impact of a Prompted Choice on Enrollment Rates for TSP among Servicemembers.

Based on the success of this pilot, DOD is committing to applying insights from this pilot across bases and installations with higher troop concentrations.

Thrift Savings Plan Re-Enrolment

In addition to promoting enrollment in TSP among currently non-enrolled Servicemembers, SBST also worked with DOD on a project to help already-enrolled Servicemembers remain in their plans. In January 2015, due to a change in the online military pay system, nearly 140,000 Servicemembers needed to re-enroll in their Roth TSP to avoid having their contributions suspended indefinitely.

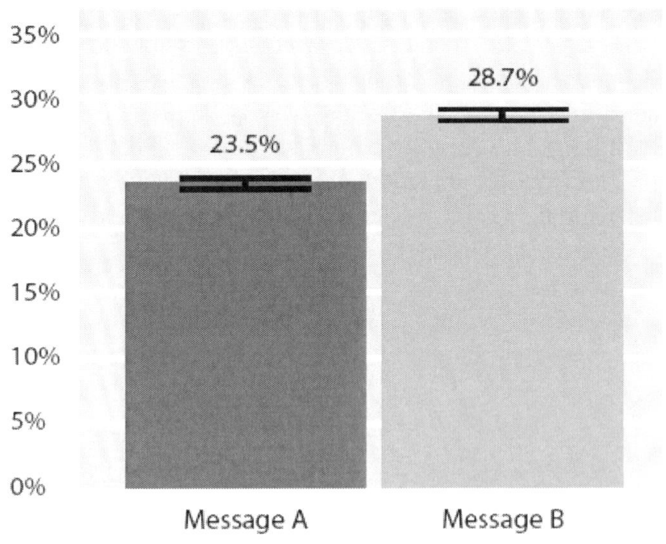

Notes: Percentage of Servicemembers re-enroiing in Roth TSP within one week after sending an email. Error bars display 95 percent confidence intervals. The difference is statisticaly significant at the 1 percent level. n = 139,273.

Figure 4. Servicemember Roth TSP Re-enrollment Rates.

Using behavioral insights, SBST redesigned DOD's standard, informational email announcing the opening of the re-enrollment window. On January 2, 2015, Servicemembers were sent either DOD's standard message or the redesigned version of the message. The redesigned message emphasized the New Year as a chance for Servicemembers to make a fresh start with their finances, clarified the three steps needed to complete the re-enrollment process, and encouraged action to avoid losing the chance to contribute savings.[18] It also included a tailored greeting ("Dear Servicemember,") and restated the key message about re-enrollment in a postscript. [19]

As shown in Figure 4, the email redesigned using behavioral insights led to a 5.2 percentage point increase (from 23.5 percent to 28.7 percent) in re-enrollments in the first week after sending the emails, representing 22 percent more Servicemembers re-enrolling in their Roth TSP. Based on this result, DOD scaled up the effective behavioral messaging in follow-up messages to all Servicemembers that encouraged Servicemembers to act before the re-enrollment deadline.

b. Improving College Access and Affordability

Having a college education has never been more important for the economic success of Americans.[20] A college degree translates into higher earnings, a lower risk of unemployment, and greater economic opportunity. At the same time, the rising costs of college have made affordability a challenge for many students and their families. SBST collaborated with the Department of Education's (ED) office of Federal Student Aid (FSA) to unlock college access for more students and help borrowers effectively manage their student loan debt.

Summer Melt

Every year, roughly 20 to 30 percent of college-accepted high school graduates in urban districts fail to matriculate in college in the fall, because they do not complete required pre-matriculation tasks such as filling out course-enrollment forms, taking placement tests, or completing the FAFSA form.[21] This phenomenon is known as "summer melt." Prior work has shown that sending students low-cost text message reminders to complete these tasks is an effective tool for curbing summer melt.[22]

In a project aimed at reducing summer melt and boosting college enrollment rates, SBST and FSA provided technical expertise to the nonprofit, college-access organization uAspire and a team of academic researchers. SBST provided feedback on the design and content of personalized text messages that reminded students to complete required pre-matriculation tasks at their intended college.[23] An example of one of the text messages is shown in Figure 5. uAspire sent a series of eight text messages informed by behavioral insights to a random sample of students over the summer months.

Notes: One of the text messages sent by uAspire as part of the summer melt intervention.

Figure 5. Example Summer Melt Text Message.

The texting intervention proved effective, boosting college enrollment by 3.1 percentage points (from 64.9 percent to 68.0 percent). The impact of the texts was particularly large for the lowest-income students, who saw a 5.7 percentage point increase in college enrollment (from 66.4 percent to 72.1 percent; see Figure 6), amounting to 8.6 percent more low-income students successfully enrolling in college.

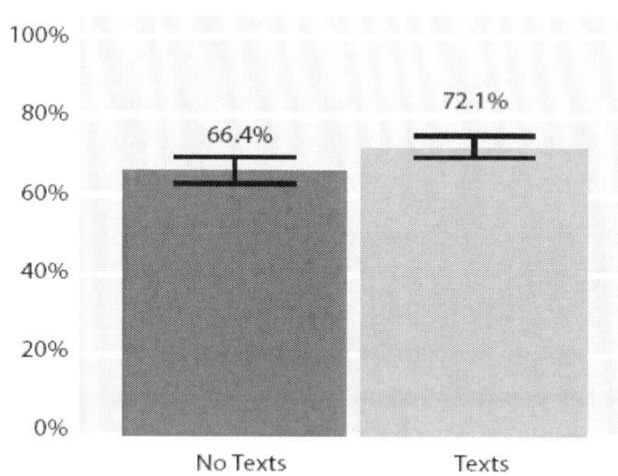

Notes: Percentage of low- income high school seniors enrolling in college in the fall of 2014. Error bars display 95 percent confidence intervals. The difference is statistically significant at the 5 percent level. n = 2,010

Figure 6. College Enrollment Rates Among Low-Income Students.

Missed Student Loan Payments

Behavioral insights can also be used to help students who have already gone to college and taken out Federal loans stay on track with their loan repayments. In one project, SBST collaborated with FSA to send email reminders to borrowers who had missed their first payments. The reminder was designed to help borrowers who were new to repayment and borrowers for whom missed payments may have been inadvertent.[24]

The email made clear that the borrower had missed a payment, sought to clarify the borrower's relationship with his or her loan servicer, and included a prominent, direct link to his or her servicer's login page. Borrowers were also directed to a link to more information about income-driven repayment plans if they could not afford their payment.

After one week the reminder email led to a 29.6 percent increase in the fraction of borrowers making a payment (from 2.7 percent to 3.5 percent). This intervention did not simply prompt people who would pay regardless to pay earlier; rather, more than three months later, the difference persisted, increasing the percentage of borrowers who made a payment from 16.0 percent to 16.6 percent. While the effects of a single email were small in absolute terms, the effects indicate that low-cost email notices and reminders can be an effective tool for promoting payment among some borrowers who fall behind.

Income-Driven Repayment Applications

For student loan borrowers who need help managing their debt, ED offers income-driven repayment (IDR) plans that link borrowers' monthly payments to their incomes. In order for these plans to have their intended impact, borrowers need to know IDR plans exist, understand the associated options and tradeoffs, and determine whether these plans are a good fit for them.

FSA, in collaboration with SBST, developed an email campaign to increase awareness of IDR and help borrowers make more-informed decisions about loan repayment options given their circumstances. In total, the campaign sent emails to more than three million struggling borrowers. SBST and FSA embedded a rigorous evaluation into the broader campaign to measure the impact of emails on 841,442 borrowers who were 90–180 days delinquent on their loans. These emails indicated IDR eligibility criteria, listed the benefits associated with taking action and the costs associated with inaction, and contained the relevant web links and servicer contact information.[25]

To evaluate the impact of sending these emails on IDR application rates, the emails were delivered to borrowers in two waves, roughly three weeks apart. Over that period, IDR application rates were four times higher among borrowers who had been sent an email than among those who had not yet been sent an email. A total of 4,327 applications for IDR were made by the former group, compared with only 982 applications by the latter.

Based on this work, SBST has collaborated with FSA to support ongoing efforts by ED to revise the IDR application form, with a focus on making it simpler and easier for student loan borrowers to complete.

Moreover, in response to the President Obama's Student Aid Bill of Rights, FSA is expanding efforts to apply behavioral insights more broadly to meet the needs of loan borrowers.[26] To continue improving outcomes for borrowers, SBST and ED are working to find the most innovative and effective ways to communicate with borrowers by leveraging the latest scientific research and identifying key factors that influence borrower repayment.[27] This effort includes a series of additional pilots that reach out to borrowers in default, borrowers who are at risk of withdrawing from school, and borrowers who are in an income-driven repayment plan and need to recertify their information each year. Results from these projects are forthcoming.

c. Advancing Economic Opportunity

The Federal Government supports economic opportunity through numerous programs and services, from job search assistance and training support, to credit programs for businesses and farmers. SBST leveraged behavioral insights to help connect Veterans with education and career counseling benefits and farmers with credit.

Education and Career Counseling Benefits for Veterans

The Department of Veterans Affairs (VA) is committed to ensuring that Servicemembers successfully reintegrate into civilian society. Through its Chapter 36 benefits program, VA offers a variety of education, training, and job placement services that empower Servicemembers to capitalize on employment opportunities.

SBST worked with VA to increase awareness of this program through low-cost informational emails. Prior to this pilot, VA did not send direct email communications to Veterans about Chapter 36 benefits. Veterans were sent one of two email variants—one highlighting Veterans' *eligibility* for the benefit and one highlighting that Veterans had *earned* the benefit through their years of service—or no email (the business-asusual practice).[28] The emails are shown in Figure 7.

Veterans Affairs Career counseling!	You've earned Veterans Affairs Career counsel-ing!
Dear [NAME], Good news! You are *eligible* for personalized career counseling from the Department of Veterans Affairs. This benefit will help you choose a career path that's right for you and take better advantage of your other VA benefits and resources.	Dear [NAME], Good news! You have *earned* personalized career counseling from the Department of Veterans Affairs. This benefit will help you choose a career path that's right for you and take better advantage of the other VA benefits and resources you've earned.

Notes: On the left, the text of the basic email containing information on the benefit; on the right, the email describing the benefits as "earned."

Figure 7. Veterans Career Benefits Emails.

The "earned" email outperformed the "eligible" email: nearly 9 percent more Veterans who were sent the "earned" email clicked through to the application than veterans who were sent the "eligible" email. But overall uptake levels remained quite low—between November 2014 (when the emails were sent) and March 2015, only a total of 146 Veterans who received an email (of either type) applied. These results suggest that barriers to enrollment in the Chapter 36 benefit program lie elsewhere.

Microloans for Farmers

Because farming often produces irregular income and requires large capital investments, the United States Department of Agriculture (USDA) offers loans to in-need farmers.

The loans are intended to benefit farmers who have difficulty obtaining credit from a commercial source and whose farms require a timely injection of capital. To meet the financing needs of small, beginning, and non-traditional farm operations, USDA's Farm Service Agency, USDA's Economic Research Service, and SBST launched an informational campaign to increase awareness and uptake of one such loan program, known as Microloans. Farmers were sent personalized letters that contained facts about Microloans, a customized set of action steps for applying, and the contact information of the recipient's local loan officer.

The informational campaign significantly increased participation in the loan program. As a result of the campaign, more farmers inquired about, applied for, and were approved for loans. In areas that received the targeted outreach, the proportion of farmers who obtained a Microloan increased by 22 percent (from 0.09 percent to 0.11 percent of farmers). USDA plans to build on this success with a second campaign this coming year.

d. Helping Families Get Health Coverage and Stay Healthy

Physical and mental health is a central element of wellbeing and carries significant social and economic implications for American society in general. A variety of Federal Government programs exist to advance the health of the Nation, including those that prevent disease, ensure food safety, offer health care to Servicemembers and Veterans, and make health insurance affordable. Programs such as Medicaid, Medicare, and, most recently, the Federal Health Insurance Marketplace, can use behavioral insights to promote access, informed decision-making, and follow-through among beneficiaries. SBST applied behavioral insights to help individuals and families obtain health insurance and stay healthy.

Federal Health Insurance Marketplace Enrolment

In one project, SBST worked with the Department of Health and Human Services' (HHS) Office of Communications to send letters to individuals who had already created an account in the Federal Health Insurance Marketplace (FHIM), but had not yet completed their application.

Health Insurance Marketplace

Dear [First name]:

You're *almost* done at HealthCare.gov — only an extra step or two needed.

You've started your online enrollment for 2015 health insurance coverage, so you already know the benefits: affordable premiums, guaranteed coverage, free preventive services, and most people qualify for financial help. And if you have any questions, quick help is available on the website or at **1-800-318-2596.** (TTY users should call 1-855-889-4325.)

But you need to act now to finish. The final deadline, February 15th, is approaching fast. **Visit HealthCare.gov** right away and complete your enrollment.

(If you've completed your enrollment already, that's great — you beat us to the punch!)

Sincerely,

Kevin Counihan
Chief Executive Officer
Health Insurance Marketplace

P.S. Don't have time this second to finish? Make a plan for when you'll act, and go stick it on your refrigerator so you don't forget!

January 2015

S	M	T	W	T	F	S
				1	2	3
4	5	6	7	8	9	10
11	12	13	14	15	16	17
18	19	20	21	22	23	24
25	26	27	28	29	30	31

February 2015

S	M	T	W	T	F	S
1	2	3	4	5	6	7
8	9	10	11	12	13	14
15						

I will complete my enrollment at HealthCare.gov on:

(name of day), (month) (day #) at (time)

Notes: This letter included a picture and implementation intention prompt at bottom for planning when to finish enrolling on the FHIM. This is variant number 4 in Figure 9.

Figure 8. Example FHIM Letter.

SBST used behavioral insights to design eight different versions of these letters, each of which prompted individuals to fi nish the application process and submit a completed application for coverage. One version, shown in Figure 8, included both a picture of the sender to grab the recipient's attenti on and personalize the message, as well as what behavioral scientists refer to as an "implementation intention prompt": an invitation to the recipient to write in the time and date at which he or she planned to return to the online exchange and complete enrollment.[29] Prior research has demonstrated that people are more likely to follow through on an intended action—such as receiving a vaccination—when they commit to taking that action at a specific moment in time.[30]

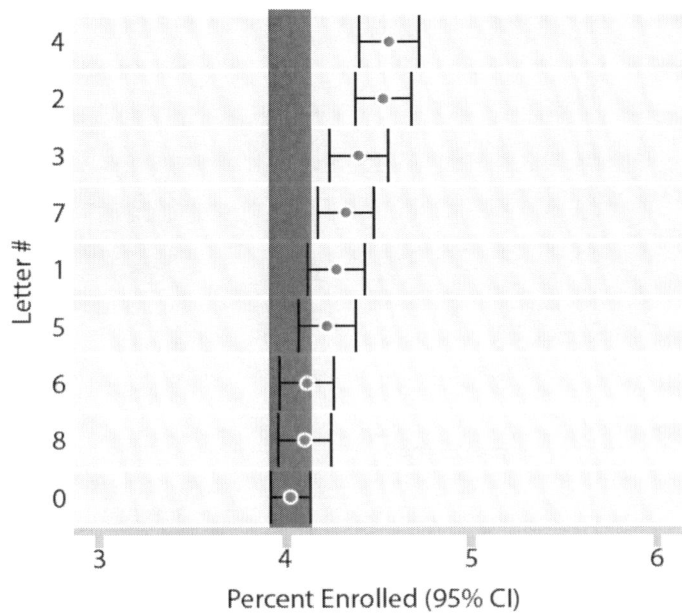

Notes: The shaded bar coincides with the 95 percent confidence interval of the group receiving no letter. n = 744,510.

Figure 9: Enrollment Rates of the Eight Letter Variant Groups, Sorted by Effectiveness.

Individuals were sent one of the eight letter variants or no letter several weeks before the open enrollment deadline. Individuals who were sent the mailer were significantly more likely to finish enrollment in a health care plan than those who were not sent a letter—a 0.3 percentage point increase. Some letters were notably more effective than others; the version that included both an implementation intention prompt and a picture of the sender boosted enrollments by 13.2 percent, while a version that had neither of these elements increased enrollments by only 1.8 percent (Figure 9).

In a closely related project, SBST and HHS worked together on an email campaign to promote FHIM enrollments. The full results of this project are forthcoming, but early findings are promising. One pilot, for instance, examined whether information about the probability of qualifying for certain tax credit benefits should be presented to individuals in terms of a percentage ("66%") or frequency ("2 out of 3"). Although the two statements are equivalent, prior work suggests that people more easily interpret frequency statements.[31] Results generated to date demonstrated that individuals sent the frequency statement were more likely to submit an application than those sent a percentage statement.

Flu Prevention

On average, the flu results in 120,000 hospitalizations and 36,000 deaths each year in the United States, yet fewer than half of Americans typically get a flu shot.[32] SBST and HHS collaborated on a project to promote vaccinations for the influenza virus among Medicare beneficiaries. During the 2014 flu season, HHS sent beneficiaries low-cost mailers informed by behavioral insights that contained information on the importance and benefits of getting vaccinated. Results of this project are forthcoming.

Global Health

Some of the most promising translations of behavioral science to health improvements have been implemented in the developing world—for example, successfully promoting chlorination of water in Kenya by making it more convenient to do so.[33] To extend the application of such findings, SBST and the United States Agency for International Development (USAID) have entered into a multi-year collaboration to use behavioral insights to improve outcomes for populations around the world. As part of this collaboration, SBST and USAID are working together on a series of pilots to promote global health. In one project, SBST is working with USAID in Mozambique to send text reminders and educational messages to patients co-infected with tuberculoisis (TB) and the human immunodeficiency virus (HIV) to boost attendance at doctors' appointments and adherence to treatment regimens. Results of this pilot are forthcoming.

III. Improving Government Efficiency

The Federal Government faces an obligation to serve the American people as efficiently as possible. This means that Federal programs should pay only qualifying individuals and for qualified expenses, and branches of Government that collect payments from individuals and businesses should receive the full amount that is owed in taxes, debts, and fees. Less-effective programs should have less claim to scarce budgetary dollars, and government operations should be free from waste.

Because these measures of government efficiency ultimately depend on the decisions and actions of individuals such as program officials, beneficiaries, and contractors, behavioral insights can improve results in this domain. For example, improving program integrity is in many cases a matter of promoting compliance with program rules. Behavioral science suggests that programs should be designed to make compliant actions salient and easy for the relevant decision makers to take.[34] When compliant behaviors become the obvious path or the path of least resistance, individuals and businesses may be more likely to pay what they owe or refrain from claiming benefits for which they do not qualify. Just as it should be easy for qualifying individuals to access programs, it should also be easy for people to play by the rules.

Behavioral insights can also improve government efficiency by providing information about which programs and opera-ti ons are more or less cost-effective. New findings about how individuals do or do not respond to programs can provide program officials with a basis for making decisions about where, or whether, to spend program dollars.

SBST used behavioral insights to generate additional collections through improved program integrity, save money on internal operational expenses, and identify programs the Government could run more effectively.

a. Promoting Program Integrity and Compliance

Program integrity and compliance are essential components of government efficiency. Integrity efforts include eliminating waste, fraud, and abuse in government programs, only paying program dollars for services or benefits according to program rules, and ensuring that programs collect all that individuals or businesses owe. Prior research from behavioral economics has demonstrated that, for example, simplifying tax collection letters and referencing the behaviors of others can accelerate tax collections. [35] SBST built on these insights to improve collections of fees from government contractors, promote repayment of non-tax debts, and encourage program compliance by medical providers.

Industrial Funding Fee Reports

SBST collaborated with the General Services Administration (GSA) to improve the accuracy of self-reported fees and collections. When the Government purchases goods and services from vendors under certain contracts, those vendors are required to do two things: first, to report those sales to the Government; and second, to pay to the Government a small fraction of their reported sales as an administrative fee, known as the Industrial Funding Fee (IFF).[36]

To promote more accurate self-reporting of the sales and, consequently, more accurate collections of IFF, SBST and GSA introduced a required signature box at the top of an online payment form for a random sample of vendors. The signature box asked vendors to confirm the truth and accuracy of the information about to be reported, as shown in Figure 10. Research indicates that requiring users to sign their names to confirm the accuracy of self-reported statements can reduce self-reporting errors if the signature is requested at the beginning of a form.[37] Interestingly, signature prompts at the end of a form seem to have no such effect.

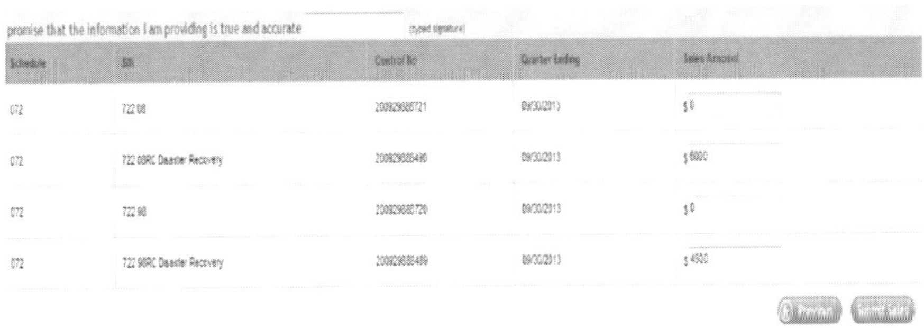
promise that the information I am providing is true and accurate

Schedule	SIN	Control No	Quarter Ending	Sales Amount
072	722 08	[illegible]	09/30/2013	$ 0
072	722 08RC Disaster Recovery	[illegible]	09/30/2013	$ 6000
072	722 98	[illegible]	09/30/2013	$ 0
072	722 98RC Disaster Recovery	[illegible]	09/30/2013	$ 4500

Notes: Screenshot of the online form where vendors self-reported sales. Those vendors required to provide the upfront signature reported significantly more in sales.

Figure 10. Industrial Funding Fee Signature Box.

The signature box was effective; the Federal Government collected an additional $1.59 million in fees within a single quarter as a result of the box. The median self-reported sales amount was $445 higher for vendors signing at the top of the form compared with those vendors who were not required to make this confirmation.

Based on this pilot result, GSA is permanently updating the online form to incorporate a signature box. SBST will also explore opportunities to apply the signature box intervention to other government contexts in which financial information is self-reported.

Delinquent Debt Repayment

In another project addressing payments, SBST worked with the Department of the Treasury's Debt Management Service (DMS) to increase collections from individuals with outstanding non-tax debt. Individuals might incur this type of debt by, for example, failing to repay Medicare for an overpayment they received. When individuals fall behind on payments of these debts by 180 days, their debt is referred to DMS. DMS then commences its own collection efforts, which include sending collection notices by mail.

Before:

You may also make an electronic payment via pay.gov: (https://www.pay.gov/paygov/forms/formInstance.html?agencyFormId=16531440)

After:

Pay online: Visit www.pay.gov/paygov/paymydebt

Notes: The text above is taken from letters redesigned using behavioral insights sent out to individuals with outstanding debt.

Figure 11. Debt Letter Web Address.

SBST and DMS used behavioral insights to redesign DMS's standard collection letter, and worked together to test the effect of the new letter compared with the original. The new letter included simplified language, a shortened web address to encourage online rather than paper payments, a personalized salutation, a prominent reference to the total amount owed in the letter's opening line, and a statement that 91 percent of Americans pay their debt on time (appealing to a social norm of timely payments).[38]

The redesigned letter was sent to a random sample of individuals with outstanding debt, and no difference in payment rates was observed between those who received the redesigned letter and those who received the standard collection letter. This may have been due to the age and status of this debt: individuals who are already 180 days or more behind in their payments may face financial barriers to repayment rather than informational barriers. Individuals sent the new letter, however, were significantly more likely to make a payment online (2.16 percent of those sent the new letter made a payment online, versus 1.49 percent of those sent the standard letter). This was likely due to the fact the web address was shortened in the new letter and was changed from a long string of meaningless characters to a shorter set of meaningful words (see Figure 11).

Based on this finding, this debt collection letter now uses the shortened form of the web address.

Prescriber Letters

A different set of program integrity and compliance efforts relate to what the Government pays as opposed to what it collects. Combating fraud, waste, and abuse is especially important in health care, where programs such as Medicare and Medicaid combine to account for nearly a quarter of all Federal spending. Applying behavioral insights to promote compliance by providers in these contexts may save costs.

One healthcare program integrity challenge is inappropriate drug prescribing, which can both threaten patient health and increase healthcare costs. The Centers for Medicare and Medicaid Services (CMS) conducts a variety of innovative practices to combat overprescribing, such as proactively identifying providers suspected of inappropriate activity and pursuing legal action through law enforcement channels.

Behavioral science research reveals a potentially cost-effective way of curbing noncompliant behavior among those who exhibit it: namely, highlighting the contrast between the actions of the individual and the social norm (how most people act). For example, households use less electricity when they are informed that their energy consumption exceeds that of their neighbors.[39] Drawing on this insight, SBST and CMS worked together on a project that sent a letter to a subset of providers with unusually high billing patterns for Schedule II prescriptions (e.g., opioids). The letter compared the provider's prescribing rates with the prescribing rates of his or her peers and provided educational information about proper prescribing practices.

This intervention had no measurable impact. Medicare drug coverage data collected 90 days after the letter was mailed showed no effect of the letter on Schedule II prescribing. SBST is currently implementing additional pilots to address over-prescription, which will improve on the initial pilot and re examine the design, timing, and frequency of letters.

b. Ensuring Cost-Effective Program Operations

Just as compliance and integrity are important for government efficiency, so too is cost-effectiveness. The Government should achieve desired outcomes by spending taxpayer dollars on programs and operations that yield positive results at reasonable costs. SBST worked on projects to identify where programs could save money by forgoing cost-ineffective measures, as well as projects to encourage cost-effective actions among government workers.

Legacy Treasury Direct Account Conversion

In one project, SBST worked with the Department of the Treasury (Treasury) on a program called Legacy Treasury Direct (LTD). LTD previously allowed investors to purchase securities such as savings bonds directly from Treasury via mail, fax, or phone. Starting in 2011, Treasury began the process of phasing out LTD in favor of TreasuryDirect, an online system.

What Should I do Next?

We've scheduled an appointment for you with your Treasury Retail Securities representative:

Please call your Treasury Retail Securities representative on *Tuesday, March 12, 2014,* between 7 am and 11 am ET, at 111-111-1111 (extension 4).

If this appointment doesn't work for you, call Monday through Friday 7 am to 4 pm ET to reschedule or walk through your account transfer today.

Notes: As part of the LTD pilot, selected individuals received a letter indicating a default call-in time.

Figure 12. Default Appointment Intervention.

Treasury and SBST worked together on a project to learn whether low-cost notices could effectively encourage LTD account holders to transition to TreasuryDirect. Account holders were randomly assigned to receive one of two letter variants designed using behavioral insights. One letter was a simplified version of letters sent in previous years. The second letter was a simplified version of previous phase-out letters, but also gave account holders a specific appointment time to call their Treasury representative. This addition draws on behavioral science research showing that individuals are more likely to follow through on plans that involve clear action steps at specific moments in time.[40] Relative to the simplified letter, the "specific appointment" letter (the relevant portion of which is displayed in Figure 12) boosted call-in rates by 2.37 percentage points. However, fewer than 5 percent of all accountholders who called in (across both letter types) said they would definitely switch to the online TreasuryDirect system.

Treasury and SBST concluded that, while it was feasible to get more investors to call in to discuss account options with representatives, these calls did not lead account holders to transition to TreasuryDirect. Treasury has no further mailings planned and is pursuing other avenues to transition analog services to digital.

Tenant Satisfaction Survey

The General Service Administration's (GSA) Public Buildings Service (PBS) owns or leases over 9,600 assets, including more than 370 million square feet of space for over a million Federal employees. Each year, PBS sends Federal employees the Tenant Satisfaction Survey (TSS), the results of which help determine Federal facilities strategy. In 2014, PBS collaborated with SBST to simplify the survey and test different messages for launching it in order to increase response rates.

SBST designed a launch email that emphasized the request ("please take the survey today!"), included a clear, mobile-optimized button linking to the survey, and had a link to a calendar invite that recipients could use to set a self-reminder to take the survey. As a result of this email, survey response rates after one week increased by about 1 percentage point (from 7.05 percent to 8 percent). Other analyses revealed how responses to the email varied by the time of day they were sent, the day of week they were sent, and across different subject lines. Among other findings, click rates were highest at lunchtime; 15.3 percent of emails sent at 11:55 a.m. saw recipients click through to the survey, compared with 13.3 percent of emails sent at 8:55 a.m.

Double-Sided Printing

In a project focused directly on the costs of government operations, SBST collaborated with USDA's Economic Research Service (ERS) to promote the use of double-sided printing among ERS employees. During a pilot period, if employees initiated a single-sided print job, a dialog box appeared that prompted individuals to change their default printer setting to double-sided, but still allowed them to continue their single-sided print job if that was preferred.

Individuals who received this prompt were more likely to print double-sided. This prompt increased the likelihood of double-sided printing on a given job by 5.8 percentage points, from a baseline of 46.0 percent. Based on this result, ERS is changing the default settings of all of its printers to double-sided.

IV. WHAT'S NEXT

SBST's inaugural year generated promising results. As detailed in this report, SBST efforts are already paying dividends for Americans. Due to SBST projects, more Service-members are saving for retirement, more students are going to college and better managing their student loans, more Veterans are taking advantage of education and career counseling benefits, more small farms are gaining access to credit, and more families are securing health insurance coverage. And improvements in government program integrity and efficiency are saving taxpayer dollars. These improvements were generated at little to no administrative cost.

Based on results from early SBST pilots, a number of agencies are already starting to make lasting changes to program design and administration. SBST will continue to work with agencies to take the lessons from these early successes to scale, so that more Servicemembers, more students, more farmers—and more Americans from all walks of life—can benefit from a Government that makes full use of the insights that behavioral science can offer. To do so, SBST will continue to help build capacity within agencies to effectively and independently apply behavioral insights to their programs.

Finally, SBST results further demonstrate the potential of behavioral insights to strengthen future policy reform efforts. If prompting enrollment at key points can boost participation in a retirement savings plan, what might that mean for the way access to that plan should be designed? If a single email can help individuals choose a student loan repayment program, what does that suggest about the way that choice set should be structured? Through small changes to program administration, the impact of SBST projects point to broader opportunities for policymakers to use behavioral insights to achieve policy goals across the Federal Government and better serve Americans.

Other SBST Efforts

In addition to projects related to streamlining program access and improving government efficiency, SBST worked to identify promising research insights from the social and behavioral sciences that informed agency policy agendas, inspired collaborations with the private sector, and contributed to existing policy processes.

Increasing opportunities for low-income children by bridging the word gap

During the first few years of life, a child from a low-income family hears millions of fewer words than her more affluent peers.[1] This deficit, known as the *word gap*, is associated with disparities in vocabulary size and, critically, school readiness.[2] Fortunately, social science has shed light on one low-cost solution: providing parents with behavioral reminders and feedback on how to improve the frequency and quality of interactions with their babies. Every time parents talk, sing, or read to their baby, it makes it easier for their baby to learn later, as heightened language input protects the brain from the pruning of unused neural connections.[3] To help bridge the word gap, OSTP, ED, HHS, and the Institute of Museum and Library Services worked with *Too Small to Fail* and the *Urban Institute* on an event that showcased innovative Federal, state, and local efforts to tackle this important problem. The event generated a series of commitments, including a technology incentive prize to inspire new behavioral tools for low-income parents, and a national research network grant to empower the research community to answer pressing questions about how to most effectively bridge the word gap.[4]

Empowering students to reach their ful potential through learning and belonging mindsets

Research demonstrates that brief interventions that teach students their minds are like muscles that can grow with hard work and perseverance, as compared to fixed traits like eye color, can increase student achievement, with the greatest gains seen for low-achieving students and females in STEM fields.[5] Research also shows that brief social belonging interventions—in which older classmates share stories of their own struggles and hardships with younger students, as well as a roadmap to success—improve resilience and persistence in college among these younger students.[6] OSTP, in collaboration with the Domestic Policy Council (DPC), the Raikes Foundation, and the Hewlett Foundation, convened experts and practitioners over the past year to advance basic research and promote effective applications to policy. As a result of these efforts, researchers at Stanford University and the University of Texas at Austin have announced the largest-ever study of learning mindset interventions at over 100 high schools nationwide. The College Transition Collaborative, a partnership of researchers and 17 colleges and universities, delivered and evaluated belonging interventions with approximately 40,000 incoming college students throughout summer 2015.[7]

Promoting the use of evidence in Federal policymaking and program administration

For the Federal Government to make responsible and effective decisions about policy design and program administration, policymakers need good evidence about what works and what does not. Findings from the behavioral sciences only reinforce the importance of basing policy design on rigorous, relevant, and up-to-date evidence (see "Behavioral Insights and the Role of Evidence"). SBST is collaborating with DPC, the Office of Management and Budget (OMB), OSTP, and the Council of Economic Advisers (CEA) as part of a coalition to promote the more effective use of evidence and evaluation at the Federal level. These efforts are currently in progress, and will result in guidance to agencies on the use of evidence to inform program decisions.

Using behavioral insights to streamline government forms

To assist with the implementation of the aforementioned Executive Order, the Office of Information and Regulatory Affairs (OIRA) and OSTP are issuing new guidance that will help Federal agencies use behavioral science insights to improve Federal forms. A burdensome, complex form can pose more than just an inconvenience to Americans: it can actually inhibit Americans from accessing a program or benefit. SBST will provide behavioral insights support to agencies on forms that: (1) reach a large number of Americans; (2) are required to access government services; and (3) currently take a long time to complete. SBST will also help agencies on forms that present operational concerns such as high error rates.

[1]Betty Hart and Todd R. Risley, *Meaningful Differences in the Everyday Experience of Young American Children*, (Baltimore, MD: Brookes, 1995). [2]Jeanne Brooks-Gunn, Cecilia E. Rouse, and Sara McLanahan, "Racial and Ethnic Gaps in School Readiness," in *School Readiness and the Transition to Kindergarten in the Era of Accountability*, ed. R.C. Pianta, M.J. Cox, and K.L. Snow, 283–306 (Baltimore, MD: Brookes, 2007). [3]Peter R. Huttenlocher, *Neural Plasticity: The Effects of Environment on the Development of the Cerebral Cortex*, (Harvard University Press, 2002).

[4]See: www.whitehouse.gov/sites/default/files/microsites/ostp/federal_ word_ gap_fact_sheet_final.pdf

[5]David S. Yeager and Gregory M. Walton, "Social-Psychological Interventions in Education: They're Not Magic," *Review of Educational Research*, 81 (2011): 267–301. David Paunesku, Gregory M. Walton, Carissa Romero, Eric N. Smith, David S. Yeager, and Carol S. Dweck, "Mindset Interventions Are a Scalable Treatment for Academic Underachievement," *Psychological Science*, 26 (2015): 784–793. Catherine Good, Joshua Aronson, and Michael Inzlicht, "Improving Adolescents' Standardized Test Performance: An Intervention to Reduce the Effects of Stereotype Threat," *Journal of Applied Developmental Psychology*, 24 (2003): 645–662.

[6]Gregory M. Walton, "The New Science of Wise Psychological Interventions," *Current Directions in Psychological Science*, 23 (2014): 73–82. Gregory M. Walton and Geoffrey L. Cohen, "A Brief Social-Belonging Intervention Improves Academic and Health Outcomes Among Minority Students," *Science* 331 (2011): 1447–1451. 7www.whitehouse.gov/the-press-office/2015/03/23/fact-sheet-president-obama-announces-over-240-million-new-stem-commitmen.

APPENDIX A: EXECUTIVE ORDER

Executive Order Using Behavioral Science Insights to Better Serve the American People

A growing body of evidence demonstrates that behavioral science insights – research findings from fields such as behavioral economics and psychology about how people make decisions and act on them – can be used to design government policies to better serve the American people.

Where Federal policies have been designed to reflect behavioral science insights, they have substantially improved outcomes for the individuals, families, communities, and businesses those policies serve. For example, automatic enrollment and automatic escalation in retirement savings plans have made it easier to save for the future, and have helped Americans accumulate billions of dollars in additional retirement savings. Similarly, streamlining the application process for Federal financial aid has made college more financially accessible for millions of students.

To more fully realize the benefits of behavioral insights and deliver better results at a lower cost for the American people, the Federal Government should design its policies and programs to reflect our best understanding of how people engage with, participate in, use, and respond to those policies and programs. By improving the effectiveness and efficiency of Government, behavioral science insights can support a range of national priorities, including helping workers to find better jobs; enabling Americans to lead longer, healthier lives; improving access to educational opportunities and support for success in school; and accelerating the transition to a low-carbon economy.

NOW, THEREFORE, by the authority vested in me as President by the Constitution and the laws of the United States, I hereby direct the following:

Section 1. Behavioral Science Insights Policy Directive.

(a) Executive departments and agencies (agencies) are encouraged to:

(i) identify policies, programs, and operations where applying behavioral science insights may yield substantial improvements in public welfare, program outcomes, and program cost effectiveness;

(ii) develop strategies for applying behavioral science insights to programs and, where possible, rigorously test and evaluate the impact of these insights;

(iii) recruit behavioral science experts to join the Federal Government as necessary to achieve the goals of this directive; and

(iv) strengthen agency relationships with the research community to better use empirical findings from the behavioral sciences.

(b) In implementing the policy directives in section (a), agencies shall:

(i) identify opportunities to help qualifying individuals, families, communities, and businesses access public programs and benefits by, as appropriate, streamlining processes that may otherwise limit or delay participation—for example, removing administrative hurdles, shortening wait times, and simplifying forms;

(ii) improve how information is presented to consumers, borrowers, program beneficiaries, and other individuals, whether as directly conveyed by the agency, or in setting standards for the presentation of information, by considering how the content, format, timing, and medium by which information is conveyed affects comprehension and action by individuals, as appropriate;

(iii) identify programs that offer choices and carefully consider how the presentation and structure of those choices, including the order, number, and arrangement of options, can most effectively promote public welfare, as appropriate, giving particular consideration to the selection and setting of default options; and

(iv) review elements of their policies and programs that are designed to encourage or make it easier for Americans to take specific actions, such as saving for retirement or completing education programs. In doing so, agencies shall consider how the timing, frequency, presentation, and labeling of benefits, taxes, subsidies, and other incentives can more effectively and efficiently promote those actions, as appropriate. Particular attention should be paid to opportunities to use nonfinancial incentives.

(c) For policies with a regulatory component, agencies are encouraged to combine this behavioral science insights policy directive with their ongoing review of existing significant regulations to identify and reduce regulatory burdens, as appropriate and consistent with Executive Order 13563 of January 18, 2011, (Improving Regulation and Regulatory Review) and Executive Order 13610 of May 10, 2012, (Identifying and Reducing Regulatory Burdens).

Sec. 2. Implementation of the Behavioral Science Insights Policy Directive.

(a) The Social and Behavioral Sciences Team (SBST), under the National Science and Technology Council (NSTC) and chaired by the Assistant to the President for Science and Technology, shall provide agencies with advice and policy guidance to help them execute the policy objectives outlined in section 1 of this order, as appropriate.

(b)The NSTC shall release a yearly report summarizing agency implementation of section 1 of this order each year until 2019. Member agencies of the SBST are expected to contribute to this report.

(c)To help execute the policy directive set forth in section 1 of this order, the Chair of the SBST shall, within 45 days of the date of this order and thereafter as necessary, issue guidance to assist agencies in implementing this order.

Sec. 3. General Provisions.

(a) Nothing in this order shall be construed to impair or otherwise affect:

(i) the authority granted by law to a department or agency, or the head thereof; or

(ii) the functions of the Director of the Office of Management and Budget relating to budgetary, administrative, or legislative proposals.

(b) This order shall be implemented consistent with applicable law and subject to the availability of appropriations.

(c) Independent agencies are strongly encouraged to comply with the requirements of this order.

(d) This order is not intended to, and does not, create any right or benefit, substantive or procedural, enforceable at law or in equity by any party against the United States, its departments, agencies, or entities, its officers, employees, or agents, or any other person.

THE WHITE HOUSE

Appendix B: Project Abstracts

SBST seeks, where feasible and cost-effective, to implement applications of behavioral insights to Federal policies and programs as demonstration projects, in order to generate evidence about the effectiveness of these applications and learn what works, what works best, and what does not work. Often, these projects implement and evaluate the impact of behavioral insights directly within Federal Government programs using rapid, rigorous, and low-cost methods (for more, see "Behavioral Insights and the Role of Evidence").

The project abstracts collected below provide additional information on the design of, and results from, projects completed by SBST through mid-2015. Wherever possible, SBST implemented these projects as randomized trials. Where random assignment proved infeasible, SBST sought to derive credible estimates of effects using the best, most practical non-experimental identification techniques applicable in each circumstance. Specific methods for each project are detailed below.

The abstracts below mirror the order of their presentation in the report, and include:

Servicemember TSP Enrollment
On-Base Servicemember TSP Enrollment
Servicemember Roth TSP Re-Enrollment
Summer Melt
Missed Student Loan Payments
Income-Driven Repayment
Education and Career Counseling Benefits for Veterans
Microloans for Farmers
Federal Health Insurance Marketplace Enrollment
Industrial Funding Fee Reports
Delinquent Debt Repayment
Prescriber Letters
Legacy Treasury Direct Accounts
Tenant Satisfaction Survey Response
Double-Sided Printing

Servicemember TSP Enrollment

Clear Action Steps, Presenting Choices, and Emphasizing Benefits Promote Savings Enrollment

Agency Objective. Increase enrollment in Thrift Savings Plans among interested active duty Servicemembers using behaviorally designed email communications.

Background. The Federal Government operates a workplace savings program called the Thrift Savings Plan (TSP) for all of its employees.[41] While the Federal Government automatically enrolls its civilian employees in TSP, it does not automatically enroll Servicemembers, and military enrollment rates average roughly 42 percent.[42] In order to enroll, Servicemembers need to log in to the Department of Defense's (DOD) Defense Finance and Accounting Service (DFAS) MyPay website and select a contribution percentage. As TSP savings through traditional (pre-tax) or Roth (after-tax) contributions can confer both short- and long-term benefits, many of the over 800,000 unenrolled Servicemembers might choose to enroll in TSP if actively presented with a chance to do so.

Methods. DFAS, in collaboration with the Social and Behavioral Sciences Team (SBST) and academic researchers, tested the impact on TSP enrollment of sending unenrolled Servicemembers emails that highlighted the opportunity and potential benefits of TSP.[43] In addition to a no-email control and a standard message drawn from TSP and DFAS web materials, eight different messages utilized different combinations of behavioral insights: clear action steps, fresh-start messaging, presentation of the decision to enroll in TSP as a choice between two options, and emphasis on short- and long-term benefits.[44] The 806,861 Service-members who were not enrolled in TSP as of April 27 were assigned to these ten groups based on the last two digits of their Social Security Number (SSN). After DFAS sent out the emails on April 29, 2015 (May 4 for Marines), it tracked TSP enrollment by SSN.

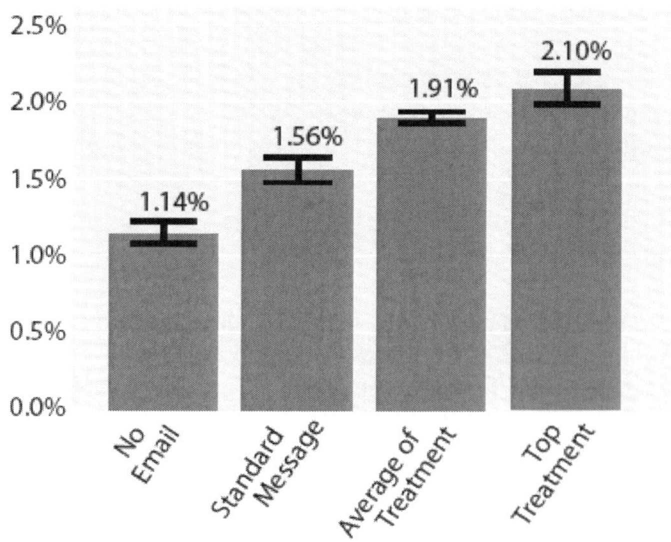

Results. One month after the emails were sent, 14,491 Servicemembers had enrolled: 920 in the no-email group (1.14 percent), compared with 1,255 sent a standard message (1.56 percent) and 12,316 across those sent the eight treatment emails (1.91 percent). The most effective email clarified the action steps needed to enroll and emphasized the potential longterm benefits of saving even a little each month. The increase in enrollment rates due to the standard email was 0.42 percentage point ($p < 0.01$, 95% CI [0.30, 0.53]), compared with 0.77 percentage point for treatment emails ($p < 0.01$, 95% CI

[0.69, 0.85]). This means that 67 percent more Servicemembers—4,930—enrolled in TSP in May 2015 as a result of being sent a treatment message.

Conclusions. Informational email campaigns are effective at prompting Servicemember enrollment in TSP, especially when designed based on behavioral insights. Lessons about which messages were most effective at motivating Servicemember action are being used to inform future outreach efforts that continue to support Servicemembers, and may help to inform future reforms to other elements of the military compensation and retirement system currently under consideration.[45]

On-Base Servicemember TSP Enrollment

Prompted Choice during a Reset Moment Promotes Savings Enrollment

Agency Objective. Actively presenting Servicemembers with a choice to enroll in Thrift Savings Plans (TSP), in order to promote enrollment.

Background. The Federal Government, including the military, operates a savings program for its employees known as the Thrift Savings Plan (TSP). Roughly 58 percent of the over 1.3 million active duty Servicemembers in the Armed Forces are not currently enrolled in any TSP plan, and only around 1 percent of non-enrolled Servicemembers newly enroll each month. The success of "prompted choice" interventions in other workplace savings contexts—where employees have to actively choose whether to contribute or not—suggests that many Servicemembers might enroll if prompted.[†] Because Permanent Change of Duty Station (PCS), or transferring to a new location, is often tied to changes in compensation and duties, in-processing briefings are a natural reset moment during which Servicemembers may benefit from prompts to make a financial decision.

Methods. In collaboration with the Department of Defense, the Social and Behavioral Sciences Team (SBST) designed a cover sheet for the TSP-U-1 Thrift Savings Plan Election Form that (a) provided information on benefits of TSP investing, and (b) actively prompted Servicemembers to contribute—or not—to TSP. The cover sheet was included in the in-processing package at Ft. Myer in Arlington, VA, and briefed Servicemembers were required to submit

[†] Previously cited as notes 16 & 17: Punam Anand Keller, Bari Harlam, George Loewenstein, and Kevin G. Volpp, "Enhanced Active Choice: A New Method to Motivate Behavior Change," Journal of Consumer Psychology 21 (2011): 376–383; Gabriel D Carroll, James J. Choi, David Laibson, Brigitte C. Madrian, and Andrew Metrick, "Optimal Defaults and Active Decisions," Quarterly Journal of Economics 124 (2009): 1639–1674.

the completed cover sheet along with other required paperwork. Briefing logistics made random assignment infeasible; for purposes of estimating impacts of the treatment period at Ft. Myer, TSP enrollment data was collected on enrollment rates at Ft. Myer over the year preceding the pilot period and from a comparison set of comparable forts: Fts. Belvoir, Bragg, and Meade.

Results. TSP enrollment rates for Servicemembers in-processed and not already enrolled at Ft. Myer during the pilot period were 8.71 percent, compared to 2.91 percent in the other three forts (Belvoir, Bragg, and Meade) during the same period. During the same date range one year prior to the pilot in 2014 (4/20/14– 6/12/14), and over a comparable length window 53 days prior to the pilot period (2/23/15–4/17/15), the average enrollment rate at Ft. Myer was 4.34 percent compared with an average of 2.88 percent at the other three forts. Using a difference-in-difference estimate, the pilot is estimated to have led to a 4.3 percentage point increase in the rate of TSP enrollment among unenrolled Servicemembers ($p < 0.05$, 95% CI [0.26, 8.42]).

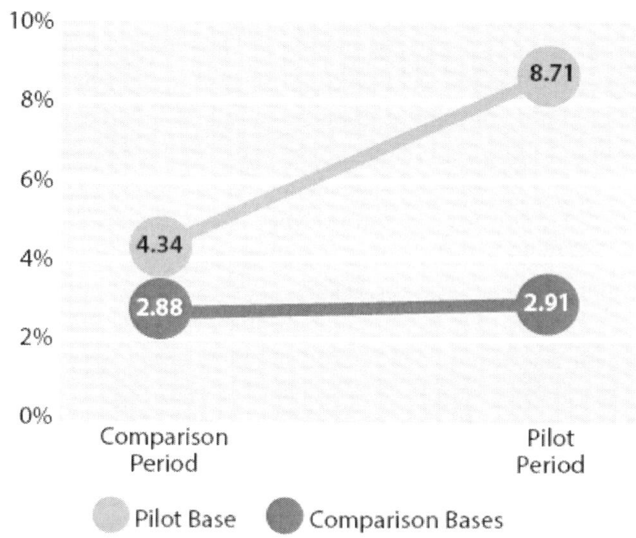

Conclusions. While auto-enrollment and auto-escalation savings plans have shown dramatic success at increasing participation in savings plans by new employees, prompted choice interventions can also be used to increase participation by existing employees through finding reset moments. These findings can inform broader policy discussions regarding defined contribution savings participation in the armed forces and beyond.

Servicemember Roth TSP Re-Enrollment

A "Fresh Start," Action-Oriented Communication Encourages Servicemember Re-Enrollment

Agency Objective. Increase re-enrollments in Roth Thrift Savings Plans among interested Servicemembers, using action-oriented, simplified email communications.

Background. Due to a change in the military pay system, 139,273 members of the Armed Forces needed to re-enroll in their Roth Thrift Savings Plans (TSP) in January 2015 to avoid having their contributions suspended indefinitely. To re-enroll, Servicemembers needed to log in to the Department of Defense's (DOD) Defense Finance and Accounting Service (DFAS) MyPay website and select a contribution percentage. DFAS conducted a broad media and email campaign to encourage affected Servicemembers to re-enroll in TSP.

Methods. As part of this campaign, DFAS, in collaboration with the Social and Behavioral Sciences Team (SBST), redesigned the standard email sent by DFAS to Servicemembers announcing the opening of the re-enrollment window. The redesigned, simplified email emphasized the New Year as a fresh start, laid out the three steps needed to complete the re-enrollment process, and encouraged action in order to avoid losing the chance to contribute savings.[46] The 139,273 Servicemembers were assigned to two groups based on the last two digits of their Social Security Number (SSN), with those with SSNs ending in 0–49 ($n = 69{,}318$) sent the standard email, and Servicemembers with SSNs ending in 50–99 ($n = 69{,}955$) sent the redesigned email. After sending the emails on January 2, 2015, DFAS tracked re-enrollment requests by SSN.

Results. One week after the emails were sent, 16,291 Servicemembers who were sent the standard email (23.5 percent) had re-enrolled, compared with 20,061 Servicemembers who were sent the redesigned email (28.7 percent). Because the last four digits of SSNs are effectively randomly assigned, the increase in re-enrollment rates of 5.2 percentage points ($p < 0.01$, 95% CI [4.7, 5.6]) can be attributed to the redesigned email. This means that 22 percent more Servicemembers—3,770—re-enrolled in their Roth TSP, or at least accelerated their re-enrollment, as a result of being sent the redesigned email instead of the standard email.

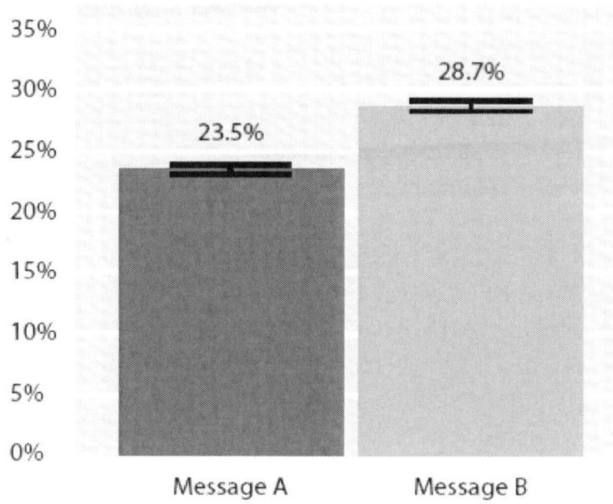

Conclusions. Because the redesigned email was more effective at prompting re-enrollment after one week, a modified version of the more effective message was subsequently scaled to the entire population in follow-up messages that encouraged Servicemembers to act before the deadline. Thus, in addition to demonstrating the relative impact of using behavioral messaging to drive action, this project also illustrates the rapid scalability of insights identified as effective via this type of rapid low cost pilot.

Summer Melt

Text Messages Reminding High School Seniors of Key Tasks Boost College Enrollment

Agency Objective. Increase college enrollment rates among college-accepted high school graduates by sending them text message reminders to complete required pre-matriculation tasks over the summer.

Background. Every year 20–30 percent of college-accepted high school graduates in urban districts fail to matriculate in college in the fall—a phenomenon known as "summer melt."[47] In the summer of 2014, the Department of Education's (ED) office of Federal Student Aid (FSA), along with the Social and Behavioral Sciences Team (SBST), provided technical expertise to the non-profit organization uAspire and a team of researchers on a text messaging campaign to students and their parents.[48] Text messages were personalized for each student and reminded each student of tasks she needed to complete to successfully matriculate. The text messages also provided recipients with a connection to individualized college and financial aid advising.

Methods. High school students from five cities participated in the pilot (n = 4,882). Students were randomly assigned to one of three groups: (1) a control group that was not sent messages; (2) a group in which only students were sent messages; (3) a group in which both students and their parents were sent messages. Prior work has shown that sending students low-cost text message reminders to complete pre-matriculation tasks is an effective tool for curbing summer melt.[49] The text message campaign began in late June and continued through late August 2014. The research team obtained student-level demographic and academic achievement data from uAspire and student-level college enrollment information from the National Student Clearinghouse.

Results. Among all students sent text messages, 68.0 percent enrolled in college in the fall compared with 64.9 percent of those not sent messages—a difference of 3.1 percentage points ($p < 0.05$, 95% CI [0.4, 5.8]). Enrollment effects were larger for the lowest-income students and for first-generation students. Among students with an expected family contribution of $0, for example, the text messages increased college enrollment by 5.7 percentage points ($p < 0.01$, 95% CI [1.4, 10.0]), from 66.4 percent to 72.1 percent. The differences between the students-only and students-and-parents treatment groups were not statistically significant.

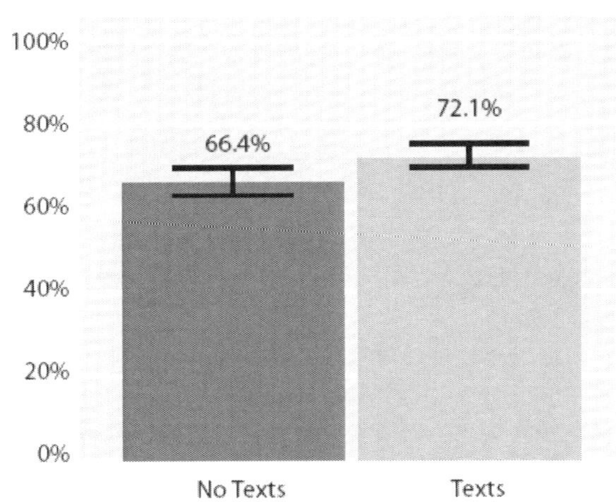

Conclusions. These findings underscore the importance of supporting college-intending high school students during the summer months leading up to the start of college, as well as the efficacy of personalized text messaging as a strategy to help students successfully matriculate in college.

Missed Student Loan Payments

Reminders Help Student Loan Borrowers Get Back on Track with Payments

Agency Objective. Help student loan borrowers who miss payments get on track with their payments using email reminders sent directly from Federal Student Aid.

Background. Federal student loan borrowers who miss their initial loan payments are in danger of defaulting on their loan.[50] To assist these borrowers, the Department of Education's (ED) office of Federal Student Aid (FSA), in collaboration with the Social and Behavioral Sciences Team (SBST), ran an email campaign to determine whether having FSA send reminder emails to borrowers—in addition to the communications from loan servicers they already receive—could help borrowers get back on track after missing their initial payments. A reminder email of this kind could particularly help those borrowers who are unaware that payments are now due or lack clarity about how to make payments.

Methods. The email campaign took place in the last week of February 2015, targeting borrowers who had missed the first or first and second payment on their monthly loan (n = 149,115). The email made clear that the borrower had missed a payment, sought to clarify the borrower's relationship with their loan servicer, and included a prominent, direct link to their servicer's login page to help with making a payment. Evidence from other contexts suggests that low-cost reminders of this nature can help individuals to make payments.[51] A link to more information about income-driven repayment (IDR) plans was also included, to which borrowers were directed if they could not afford their payment.

The project proceeded in two phases: In the first, FSA identified an effective subject line by randomly sending different subject lines to four groups of 12,500 borrowers each and comparing open rates. (The line "You missed a payment on your Federal student loan" was most effective by this measure). In the second phase, emails using the winning subject line were sent to a randomly selected set of the remaining borrowers (n = 77,115). A control group (n = 22,000) did not receive any communications from FSA, but continued to receive any ongoing communications from their loan servicers. Payment rates for all groups were tracked through the end of June 2015.

Results. In the seven days after the emails were sent, 3.5 percent of borrowers who were sent an email made at least one payment compared to 2.7 percent of the control group—a difference of 0.8 percentage points ($p < 0.01$, 95% CI [0.6, 1.0]). This difference persisted: more than three months after the emails were sent, the fraction of those groups having made a payment had risen to 16.6 and 16.0 percent, respectively, a difference of 0.6 percentage point ($p < 0.05$, 95% CI [0.1, 1.1]). There were no significant differences in the number of IDR applications; however, borrowers who received emails were less likely to access FSA's repayment calculator ($p < 0.01$) or to switch to deferment or forbearance on their loans ($p < 0.01$).

Conclusions. Emails that reminded student loan borrowers about missed payments and clarified how to make a payment led to significantly, but modestly, higher payment rates for the treatment group, and these higher rates persisted throughout the follow-up period.

Income-Driven Repayment

Notifications to Borrowers About Income-Driven Repayment (IDR) Plans Increase Application Rates

Agency Objective. Increase applications for income-driven repayment plans among delinquent student loan borrowers with email notices designed using behavioral insights.

Background. As student loan balances have risen in recent years, an increasing numbers of borrowers have struggled to stay on track with their payments.[52] At-risk and delinquent borrowers may benefit from income-driven repayment (IDR) options, which link monthly payment amounts to their incomes, and can make repayment more manageable.[53] However, enrolling in an IDR plan requires that borrowers learn of and apply for such a plan. In late 2013, the office of Federal Student Aid (FSA) within the Department of Education (ED), in collaboration with the Social and Behavioral Sciences Team (SBST), conducted an email campaign to help at-risk student loan borrowers learn of and apply for these alternative payment plans.

Methods. Borrowers who were 90 to 180 days delinquent (n = 841,442) were randomly assigned along two, independent dimensions. First, the timing of the email was varied so that half of the sample was sent the email in

November and half in December 2013. Second, the format and content of the email were varied, comparing four variants designed using behavioral insights: a longer, more comprehensive email; a shorter and less-detailed version of the email; a loss-framed email; and a gain-framed email.[54]

Results. Emails had a significant, positive impact on completed IDR applications. Of those borrowers who were sent an email, 1.02 percent submitted an IDR application in the 20 days following the email, compared with only 0.23 percent of those not sent the email, a difference of 0.79 percentage point ($p < 0.01$, 95% CI [0.75, 0.82]). Across variants, the longer email was slightly more effective at prompting IDR applications. Borrowers sent the longer email completed applications at a rate of 1.04 percent in the 20 days after sending, compared with 0.86 percent of those sent the shorter email ($p < 0.01$, 95% CI [0.12, 0.24]). The loss-framed email was slightly more effective at leading to applications than the gain-framed email, but each was less effective than the more comprehensive, longer email (all differences $p < 0.05$).

Conclusions. These findings suggest that low-cost, timely notices can make a significant difference on IDR enrollment rates among struggling student loan borrowers. While the effects are small in size in relative terms, this outcome is a measure of application rates within a twenty-day window following a single email. Given the large population of at-risk and delinquent borrowers, the absolute effect is substantial: the results suggest that sending just a single email led roughly 6,600 additional borrowers to sign up for an IDR plan.

Education and Career Counseling Benefits for Veterans

Communications Emphasizing That Benefits Are Earned through Their Service to Encourage Veterans to Apply and Enroll for an Education and Career Counseling Benefit

Agency Objective. Increase the take-up of education and career counseling benefits among interested Veterans using email outreach designed using behavioral insights.

Background. The Department of Veterans' Affairs (VA) is committed to help military Servicemembers fully reintegrate back into society through educati on, training, and career counseling programs.[55] VA's Chapter 36 Education and Career Counseling benefit (Chapter 36) is a reintegration service provided by VA's Vocational Rehabilitation and Education office

(VR&E). Chapter 36 services include personalized counseling on education, career options, and accessing related VA benefits.[56] The Chapter 36 application process is paper-based and involves multiple steps, which may create barriers to access.

Methods. VR&E, in collaboration with the Social and Behavioral Sciences Team (SBST) and academic researchers, identified email as a low cost tool to inform Veterans about Chapter 36 benefits, their eligibility, the application process, and what to expect after an application was submitted.[57] Eligible Veterans with a valid email address on record were randomly assigned to one of three conditions:[58] (1) *Business as usual*: sent no email from the VA about the benefit ($n = 21{,}423$); (2) *Basic email*: sent an email that explained they were eligible for free career counseling and provided a link to download the application form ($n = 21{,}424$); and (3) *Earned*: sent an email otherwise identical to the basic email, but with an emphasis on the fact that Veterans had earned the benefit through their service ($n = 21{,}423$).[59] To measure the impact of the emails, four outcomes were tracked using existing VA data: email open rates, click rates (on the link to the application form), applications submitted, and Veterans who completed services with counseling.

Results. The *Earned* email outperformed the *Basic* email on open (42.6 versus 40.0 percent, $p < 0.01$, 95% CI [1.6, 3.6]) and click rates (4.1 vs 3.6 percent, $p < 0.03$, 95% CI [0.11, 0.89]). The emails increased applications and completion of services with counseling measurably, but overall uptake rates remained low. Without the emails, rates of application remained near 0 (only one person in the *Business as usual* group applied for benefits during the trial period); the *Basic* email increased applications to 0.37 percent ($p < 0.01$) and the *Earned* email to 0.30 percent ($p < 0.01$). There is no meaningful difference between the two emails ($p = 0.79$).

Conclusions. These results suggest that email can be an inexpensive and effective way to share information about Chapter 36 benefits, but that they may not lead to substantial improvements in utilization. More extensive changes may be necessary to promote access to these benefits. However, communication about VA benefits should describe the benefits as those that Veterans have earned through their service.

Microloans for Farmers

Personalized Outreach to Farmers Increases Successful Small-Business Loan Applications

Agency Objective. Provide information on the USDA Microloans program to farmers.

Background. The U.S. Department of Agriculture's, (USDA) Farm Service Agency (FSA) launched the Microloan program in January 2013 to better serve the needs of small farms, beginning farmers, and farmers from historically socially disadvantaged groups.[60] As their name suggests, these loans are smaller than other direct operating loans, with an initial maximum of $35,000 that was raised to $50,000 in November 2014. The loans are designed to be more convenient and accessible to nontraditional producers who might lack the business and credit history that traditional clients of the direct operating loan program have. This includes a streamlined application process and relaxed requirements for collateral and previous experience in farming.

Methods. In collaboration with the Farm Service Agency (FSA), the USDA's Economic Research Service and SBST designed an outreach letter that provided information on the benefits of the Microloan program, personalized contact information for local loan officers, and a shortened web address for accessing more information.* The letters were sent in late April to farmers in a random sample of zip codes in nine states: Alabama, Arkansas, Georgia, Kentucky, Louisiana, Mississippi, North Carolina, South Carolina, and Tennessee. Farmers who were interested in Microloans were encouraged to follow up by calling, emailing, or visiting their local county FSA offices to discuss options with an FSA loan officer. Letters were sent to all farms in 1,848 treatment zip codes.

Results. The letter increased the number of successful applicants for Microloans. The number of farms that apply for and receive a Microloan is small compared to the overall population of farms—131 farms in control zip codes, or approximately 0.09 percent, applied for and received a Microloan between late April and July 2015. In the treatment group, that figure increased to 165 farms, or 0.11 percent of all farms in treatment zip codes, a difference of 0.02 percentage point ($p < 0.05$, 95% CI [0.00, 0.05]).

Consistent with this result, data collected by FSA on activity at county offices indicate that the letters increased the amount of Microloan-related activity in FSA county offices. Approximately 1.8 percent of the recorded activity in FSA county offices from late April through July of 2015 had to do with Microloans. Of those customers who gave information about themselves when they inquired about Microloans, 2.85 percent of the office activity was generated by Microloans in zip codes that did not receive letters, while 4.90 percent of the office activity was generated by Microloans in zip codes that received letters, a difference of 2.05 percentage points ($p < 0.01$).

Conclusion. Providing actionable information to new farmers can increase access to Microloan credit.

Federal Health Insurance Marketplace Enrollment

Action language, planning prompts, and personalization promote follow-through on Health Insurance Enrollment

Agency Objective. Assist uninsured Americans with completing their health insurance application in time by sending behaviorally designed letters prior to the deadline for open enrollment.

Background. During the Open Enrollment Period, qualifying individuals and families can purchase health insurance plans through the Federal Health Insurance Marketplace (FHIM).[61] For the 2015 enrollment season, the close of open enrollment was February 15, 2015. As of early February 2015, many people had visited HealthCare.gov and started an online account, but not yet selected a plan. The Department of Health and Human Services (HHS), in collaboration with the Social and Behavioral Sciences Team (SBST), developed and sent letters to assist these individuals with completing their insurance application in time.

Methods. From February 2 to 4, 2015, individuals who had registered for a HealthCare.gov user account but not yet enrolled in an insurance plan (n = 811,795) were randomly assigned to be sent one of eight letter variants or no letter at all (the “hold-out” group). The eight letters varied behavioral dynamics including action language, an implementation intention prompt, a picture, social norm messaging, a pledge, and loss aversion.[62] The core content of the letter about how to enroll (information about the benefits of enrolling, the deadline, the website link, and a phone number) was held constant across each of the eight letters.

Results. By the February 15 deadline, enrollments were 4.03 percent in the hold-out group and 4.32 percent across letter variants—a 7.15 percent increase ($p < 0.001$, 95% CI [5.89, 8.42]) amounting to 1,924 marginal enrollments. Not all letters had equal effects (see figure): the highest performing letter (#4, designed with behavioral dynamics of action language, an implementation intention, and a picture) boosted enrollments by 13.17

percent compared with only 1.84 percent for letter #8 (a "kitchen sink" variant including all dynamics minus the pledge). A social norm message (about the "millions of Americans" enrolled) in #8, 6, and 5 was ineffective.

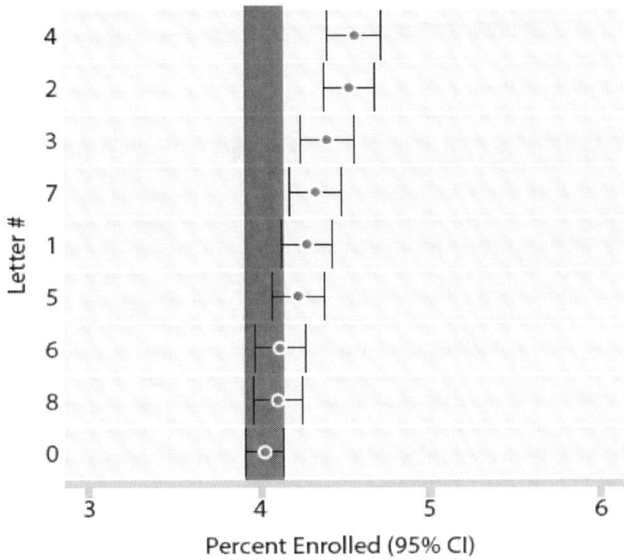

Enrollment rates of the eight letter variants, sorted by effectiveness. The shaded bar indicates the 95% confidence interval of the group that was sent no letter.

Conclusions. Letter campaigns are effective at prompting completion of health insurance applications for those who have demonstrated interest and initiated the process. This is especially the case when effort is invested in behavioral design and randomized testing to measure relative performance.

Industrial Funding Fee Reports

A Confirmation Prompt Reduces Financial Self-Reporting Error

Agency Objective. Reduce financial self-reporting errors using a redesigned data-entry form.

Background. Federal vendors are required to pay a fee, called the *industrial funding fee* (IFF), currently set at 0.75 percent of quarterly sales on certain transactions.[63] The size of the IFF payment is determined from self-reports submitted via a website (https://72a.gsa. gov/). In fiscal year 2013, the

General Services Administration (GSA) collected approximately $269 million in IFF across roughly 47,000 transactions.

The GSA, in collaboration with the Social and Behavioral Sciences Team (SBST), introduced a confirmation prompt as part of the IFF data-entry form in order to reduce financial self-reporting errors. Research has shown that inserting a confirmation prompt, where the user signs his or her name confirming the accuracy of the self-reported statements, reduces self-report errors if done at the beginning of a form; prompts at the end of a form seem to have no effect.[64]

Methods. The randomized controlled trial was fielded during the third reporting quarter of 2014, where vendors (n = 18,477) were randomly assigned to use either: (a) the existing reporting system (control); or (b) a modified interface (treatment), redesigned to include an opening signature box confirming, "I promise that the information I am providing is true and accurate." Administrative data on paid IFF provided the primary outcome measure.

Results. The median self-reported sales amount was $445 ($p < 0.05$, 95% CI [87, 803]) higher for vendors signing at the top of the form compared with those vendors who were not required to make this confirmation. The increase in IFF remittances in the treatment group in just the third quarter of 2014 was $1.59 million.

Conclusions. Confirmation prompts at the beginning of a form are a promising approach to reducing financial self-reporting errors, especially given the near-zero marginal cost to implement.

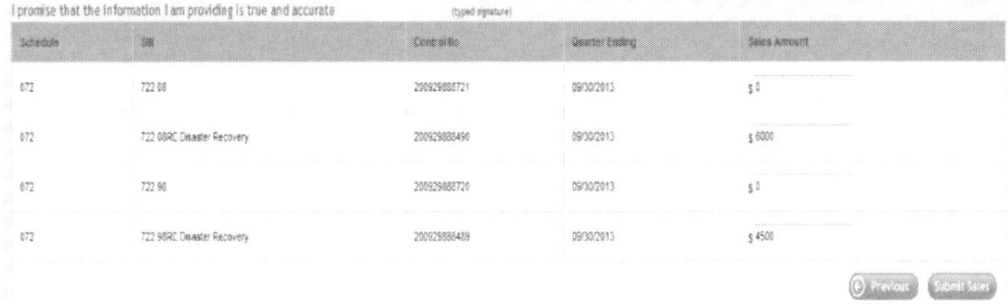

Delinquent Debt Repayment

Simplified Letters Promote Greater Use of Online Payments for Delinquent Debts

Agency Objective. Increase the rate of debt recovery by simplifying notification letters.

Background. The Department of the Treasury's Debt Management Services (DMS) collects delinquent debts from individuals who have incurred and fallen behind on non-tax debts to Federal agencies.[65] Agencies are required to refer debts to DMS at 180 days delinquent.[66] DMS collection letters are typically sent within 4 days of receiving the debt from a referring Federal agency. In 2013, DMS, in collaboration with the Social and Behavioral Sciences Team (SBST), modified its collection letter using behavioral insights to increase the rate of debt recovery.

Methods. The new letter was simplified (e.g., multiple mailing addresses linked to the Department of Treasury were removed from the letter and replaced with a single address; the web address for online payment was shortened substantially), personalized (individuals were addressed by name rather than by debt ID number), and the total debt owed was emphasized in the letter's opening line. In addition, based on recent research from the United Kingdom showing that social comparisons can increase tax collections, the new letter highlighted the fact that 91 percent of Americans pay their debt on time.[67]

To determine the effectiveness of the changes, the new letter was compared to the status quo delinquency letter during a trial conducted between October 2013 and March 2014. Individuals (n = 21,305) with debts from six creditor agencies were randomly assigned to be sent either the status quo or new letter. Three outcomes were measured at 30 and 60 days from sending: (i) receipt of payment on debts; (ii) debtor contact via inbound calls to DMS; and, (iii) debtor-initiated payments to pay.gov.

Results. No differences were found in overall payment rates or inbound calls across the letter types. Individuals were significantly more likely to make a payment via pay.gov (rather than by mail) if they were sent the new letter (2.16 versus 1.49 percent, $p < 0.05$, 95% CI [0.30, 1.04]). Some collection was made within 30 days on 5.89 percent of all debts included in the sample. There were significant differences across agencies in the proportion of all debts on which payment was received (ranging from 1.79 to 12.78 percent). Debt size was also a significant predictor of payment (smaller debts were more likely to receive payment).

Conclusions. The evidence from the trial suggests that the new letter did not affect overall payment rates on delinquent, non-tax debt. It did affect the method of payment, however, by increasing utilization of online payments.

Prescriber Letters

Letters to Providers As a Means to Promote Program Integrity in Medicare Part D

Agency Objective. Reduce inappropriate prescribing of controlled substances in Medicare Part D.[68]

Background. Inappropriate prescribing can threaten patient health and increase healthcare costs. A body of research shows evidence of some providers over-prescribing certain pharmaceuticals, including controlled substances, benzodiazepines, and antipsychotics.[69] Through its Center for Program Integrity (CPI), the Centers for Medicare and Medicaid Services (CMS) uses a variety of approaches to combat overprescribing behavior, such as proactively identifying providers suspected of inappropriate activity and pursuing legal action through law enforcement channels.

Studies have shown that letters, especially those highlighting social comparisons, can motivate individuals to more carefully examine their own behavior. Simply stating that "9 out of 10 people pay their taxes on time," for example, has been shown to substantially increase timely tax payments.[70] Physicians are more likely to provide vaccinations after receiving feedback on their vaccination rates relative to peers.[71] CPI, in collaboration with the Social and Behavioral Sciences Team (SBST) and academic researchers, developed and sent letters to providers incorporating this behavioral insight to promote program integrity in Medicare Part D.

Methods. Potential improper prescribers of Schedule II drugs (e.g., opioids) were identified as those who prescribed far more than their peers in the same state and medical specialty. These providers (n = 1,518) were randomly assigned to be sent a letter (in September 2014) or not. The letter depicted an individual's prescribing rates in comparison to his or her peers, and provided information about proper prescribing practices. The letter was designed to educate providers and induce them to "self-audit" to correct potenti ally improper payments. The effect of the letter on prescribing was tracked via Part D claims data.

Results. Using data collected over the 90 days after the letter was mailed, comparisons failed to detect an effect of the letter on Schedule II prescribing.

Tests can reject that the letter reduced prescribing by more than 1.4 percent, but cannot reject effects smaller than that—though a reduction less than 1.4 percent could be medically and economically significant.

Conclusions. The letter as designed did not exert a detectable effect. Given the low cost of letter interventions, and the fact that informative letters have been shown to work in other contexts, this finding has prompted the research team to explore alternative approaches to reaching providers as well as the design, timing, and frequency of the letters. Additional letter-based testing is currently underway.

LEGACY TREASURY DIRECT ACCOUNTS

Default Call-In Appointments Encourage Account Holder Response

Agency Objective. Determine if letters work to encourage account transfers by securities holders.

Background. The Department of the Treasury's Legacy Treasury Direct (LTD) program allowed investors to purchase marketable securities directly from the Treasury, via mail, fax, and phone.[72] The program was phased out starting in 2011, before being decommissioned in late 2014. Before and during the phase out, Treasury sent several letters to LTD account holders encouraging them to transition their accounts to, among other places, TreasuryDirect, an online system opened in 2002.

Methods. In an effort to move customers to the all-electronic system, the Bureau of the Fiscal Service (Fiscal Service) at the Treasury collaborated with the Social and Behavioral Sciences Team (SBST) to develop two letters for LTD account holders. First, a *Clarified Standard* letter, a simplified version of the previous years' letters. Second, a *Default Appointment* letter, with similar text as the first, and which also gave recipients an appointment with their Treasury representative during a low call volume time window at the Fiscal Service call center. The *Default Appointment* letter builds on behavioral science research finding that individuals are more likely to follow through on plans that identify specific moments of action.[73]

The letters were mailed to the 33,500 remaining LTD account holders over 16 business days, with each of the two letters mailed to batches of 1,000 accounts by zip code in sequential numerical order. Fiscal Service's call center collected data on LTD account holder call-in actions, including indicators for actions taken by or indicated by the caller, such as whether the caller indicated an interest in taking any account actions, and whether the caller established an online account. Using letter identification numbers printed on each letter (e.g., 9965 or 8865 in the top right corner of the letter), the type of letter (*Clarified Standard* or *Default Appointment*) was linked to data on call-in actions, which allowed for observation of differences in call-in actions by letter type.

Results. Compared with the *Clarified Standard* letter, the *Default Appointment* letter resulted in a call-in rate that was 2.37 percentage points higher ($p < 0.05$, 95% CI [1.69, 3.07]), an increase of 23 percent. Fewer than 5 percent of the LTD account holders who called in (across both treatment groups) said they would definitely switch to the online Treasury Direct system.

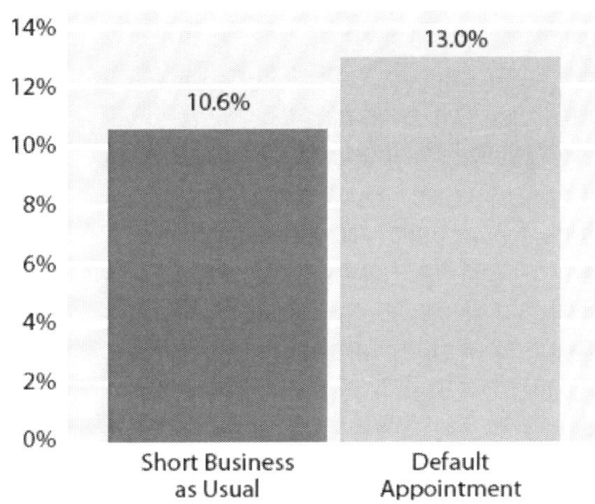

Conclusions. Creating a moment of action for calling in resulted in more investors calling in to discuss account options with Treasury representatives. However, the mailings did not result in significant customer account changes from LTD to TreasuryDirect. There are no further LTD mailings planned.

Tenant Satisfaction Survey Response: Calendar Invite

Simplification and Calendar Invitations Increase Survey Response

Agency Objective. Increase response rates in a workplace survey that directly informs Federal facility strategy.

Background. The General Service Administration (GSA)'s Public Buildings Service (PBS) owns or leases over 9,600 assets, with more than 370 million square feet of space for over a million Federal employees. Each year,

PBS sends Federal employees the Tenant Satisfaction Survey (TSS), the results of which help determine Federal facilities strategy. In 2014, PBS collaborated with the Social and Behavioral Sciences Team (SBST) to simplify the survey and test different messages for launching the survey, with the goal of increasing response rates.

Methods. Pilot TSS announcement emails were randomly assigned to a randomly selected sample of 29,997 employees at agencies using Federally owned or leased office space. A *Business as Usual* launch email was sent to 14,997 employees, with content based on the previous year's announcement materials, emphasizing that the survey was online and saved the government paper and time. A *Simplified Calendar Reminder* launch email was sent to 15,000 employees, emphasizing what the email was requesting ("please take the survey today!"); it also had a clear, mobile-optimized button linking to the survey and an embedded link to a calendar invite recipients could use to set a reminder to take the survey at the official launch time. The two emails had distinct links to two identical versions of the survey, allowing tracking of survey views, starts, and completions by email group.

Results. One week after sending the emails, the *Simplified Calendar Reminder* email resulted in a nearly 1 percentage point ($p < 0.01$, 95% CI [0.35, 1.5]) higher completion rate amongst people sent the email, a 13.5 percent higher relative completion rate. The *Simplified Calendar Reminder* also promoted survey completion conditional on starting the survey—among those who viewed and started the survey, it led to completion rates that were 3 percentage points higher ($p < 0.01$, CI [2.15, 4.25]).

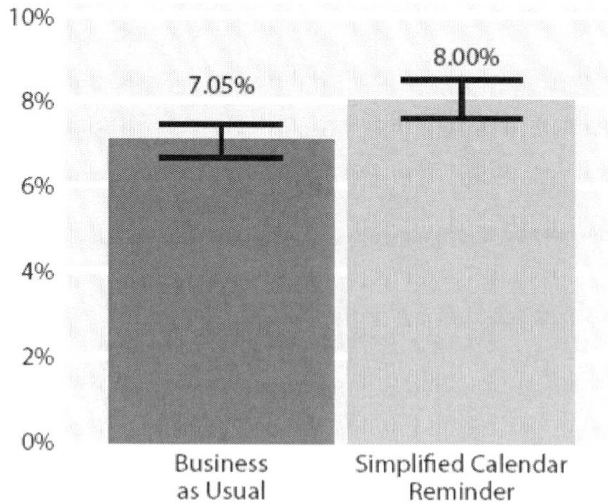

Conclusions. A simplified, clear request, with an embedded reminder and a button to easily follow through, led more people to view, begin, and complete a workplace survey. Two days following the pilot, the more successful version of the pilot launch message was sent out in the full TSS launch, helping to immediately scale insights from the pilot test to help PBS reach their goal of gathering feedback from as many Federal tenants as possible.

Tenant Satisfaction Survey Response: Time of Day

Lunchtime Emails Maximize Click and Open Rates

Agency Objective. Increase open and click rates in response to an email announcing a workplace survey.

Background. The General Service Administration (GSA)'s Public Buildings Service (PBS) owns or leases over 9,600 assets, with more than 370 million square feet of space for over a million Federal employees.[79] Each year, PBS sends Federal employees the Tenant Satisfaction Survey (TSS), the results of which help determine Federal facilities strategy. In 2014, PBS collaborated with the Social and Behavioral Sciences Team (SBST) to simplify the survey and test different messages for launching the survey, with the goal of increasing response rates.

Methods. In scaling the successful messages from the TSS launch pilot (see above, "TSS Response: Calendar Invite"), PBS spread out the full launch emails among the intended 873,755 recipients over the course of Thursday, July 10, 2014. In order to reduce burden on the survey site contractor and ensure the site operated, the same email was scheduled to be sent to randomly selected groups of 96,000 federal employees every hour over the course of the day (at 8:55 a.m., 9:55 a.m., etc.) (all send times Eastern). The response to these launch emails overloaded the survey contractor's website, and further emails were postponed following the 1:55 p.m. email (the remaining workers were sent launch emails over the following week; see below, "TSS Response: Subject Lines and Day of Week"). Data on recipient agency and location came from Office of Personnel Management (OPM) records. GovDelivery, the email service, provided data on email open and click rates.

Results. Relative to the 8:55 a.m. send, the highest email open and click rates came near noon, at the 11:55 a.m. send. Controlling for the effects of states and agency of recipients, emails sent at 11:55 a.m. had an open rate that was 2.5 percentage points higher ($p < 0.01$, 95% CI [2.16, 2.86]), and a click rate that was 1.5 percentage points higher ($p < 0.01$, 95% CI [1.19, 1.82])—that is, sending emails three hours later meant that approximately 1,500 more people read and followed through on the email request.

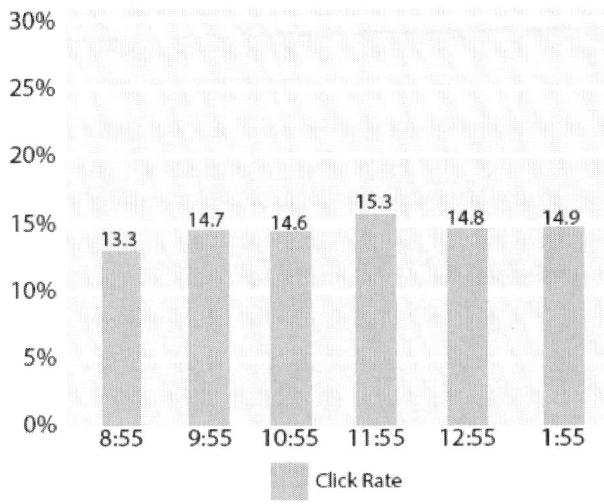

Conclusions. Lunchtime was a better time of day than 9 a.m. to send workplace survey requests to a work email address to maximize open and click rates. These lessons may be useful for other broad workplace requests. Moreover, the methods of testing different times of sending workplace email requests are more broadly applicable across the Federal Government.

Tenant Satisfaction Survey Response: Subject Lines and Day of Week

Maximizing Response to Workplace Emails by Varying Send Day, Send Time, and Subject Lines

Agency Objective. Determine what day of week and time of day is best to send emails to increase email opens and clicks; determine what subject line content and punctuation increases opens and clicks.

Background. The General Service Administration (GSA)'s Public Buildings Service (PBS) owns or leases over 9,600 assets, with more than 370 million square feet of space for over a million Federal employees.[80] Each year, PBS sends Federal employees the Tenant Satisfaction Survey (TSS), the results of which help determine Federal facilities strategy. In 2014, PBS collaborated with the Social and Behavioral Sciences Team (SBST) to simplify the survey and test different messages for launching the survey, with the goal of increasing response rates. After scaling the successful messages from the TSS launch pilot (see above, "TSS Response: Calendar Invite"), and overwhelming the survey contractor's website with a full launch (see above, "TSS Response: Time of Day"), PBS and SBST spaced out the remaining announcement population into three batches of roughly 23,000 recipients each day for seven business days.

Methods. An announcement email was sent to two randomly assigned groups of approximately 11,500 Federal employees three times a day for a week—at 9:00 a.m., 12:30 p.m., and 4:00 p.m. (all send times Eastern). In addition to time-of-day and day-of-week variation, PBS and SBST varied aspects of the subject line, testing paired permutations of the following against each other: "2014 Tenant Satisfaction Survey," "2014 Tenant Satisfaction Survey – Take it Today" and "2014 Tenant Satisfaction Survey – Please Take it Today."

The emails also varied the use of an exclamation point on each of those subject lines. Data on recipient agency and location came from Office of Personnel Management (OPM) records. GovDelivery, the email service, provided data on email open and click rates.

Results. Controlling for state and agency effects, the highest likelihoods of opens and clicks came on Tuesdays (1.8 percentage points higher open, 1.2 percentage points higher click) and Wednesdays (1.9 percentage points higher open, 1.0 percentage point higher click), relative to Fridays ($p < 0.01$). Relative to mornings, lunchtime sends had higher clicks (0.3 percentage point) and opens (0.3 percentage point) ($p < 0.01$). And relative to the lowest performing subject line ("2014 Tenant Satisfaction Survey – Take it Today") adding "Please" led to 1.0 percentage point more clicks and 0.5 percentage point more opens ($p < 0.01$); adding an exclamation point led to 0.8 percentage point fewer opens, and 0.5 percentage point fewer clicks ($p < 0.01$).

Conclusions. The findings from these TSS tests— that sending emails near lunchtime on Tuesdays and Wednesdays resulted in higher responses; and that saying "please" in subject lines helped while adding an exclamation point hurt—may not hold in every government or workplace email context. However, they provide meaningful evidence on responses to workplace requests. Perhaps more significantly, the methods and practices of testing different approaches to workplace email requests are broadly applicable across government.

Double-Sided Printing

One Small Prompt Saves Money and Resources

Agency Objective. Reduce cost and total paper use at a Federal Government agency by employing a simple, low-cost pop-up message, delivered when users print, to discourage single-sided printing.

Background. Not surprisingly given its scale, the Federal Government uses a great deal of paper. A 2009 survey indicated that the average government employee printed about 30 pages per day.[74] At 2.6 million executive branch employees and 240 working days per year, that amounts to over 18 billion pages printed per year.[75] Reliable figures on the rate of duplex printing (double-sided printing) across the government do not exist, but in data for this project the baseline rate of duplex printing was 46 percent of all print jobs, implying significant scope to reduce total paper use and reduce costs through the increased use of double-sided printing.

Methods. The Department of Agriculture's (USDA) Economic Research Service (ERS), in collaboration with the Social and Behavioral Sciences Team (SBST), tested the effectiveness of adding a small cost to printing single- rather than double-sided for its employees. Behavioral science research from other contexts suggests that even relatively minor costs associated with taking one action can be sufficient to lead individuals to take a different action.[76]

Implementation of this cost was randomized at the printer level within ERS. The small cost to printing single-sided was introduced by presenting individuals, when they attempted to print a single-sided document at a network printer in the treatment group, with a pop-up box (an image of which is displayed at right).

This pop-up required a second mouse click before single-sided printing would occur. If the individual did not click "Print" after five minutes, the print job was deleted. The text of the pop-up notified individuals that if they changed their default settings to duplex, they would not face the pop-up in the future.

Results. This simple prompt increased the likelihood of duplex printing on a given job by 5.8 percentage points ($p < 0.01$, 95% CI [4.2, 7.4]), from a baseline of 46.0 percent.

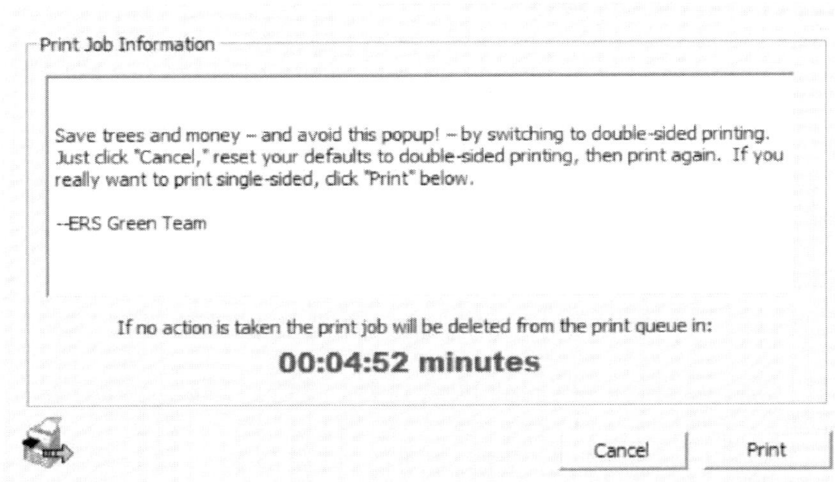

Conclusions. These results suggest that a simple message, which could easily be scaled to any networked printer using existing software, can be an inexpensive and effective way to reduce the proportion of single-sided print jobs. Based on this result, ERS is scaling up the use of the pop-up box to all its networked printers. That individuals are responsive to this intervention suggests that stronger interventions, such as changing printer defaults to double-sided printing, could be more powerful still in this context.

SOCIAL AND BEHAVIORAL SCIENCES TEAM 2015 ANNUAL REPORT

About the National Science and Technology Council

The National Science and Technology Council (NSTC) is the principal means by which the Executive Branch coordinates science and technology policy across the diverse entities that make up the Federal research and development (R&D) enterprise. One of the NSTC's primary objectives is establishing clear national goals for Federal science and technology investments. The NSTC prepares R&D packages aimed at accomplishing multiple national goals. The NSTC's work is organized under five committees: Environment, Natural Resources, and Sustainability; Homeland and National Security; Science, Technology, Engineering, and Mathematics (STEM) Education; Science; and Technology. Each of these committees oversees subcommittees and working groups that are focused on different aspects of science and technology. More information is available at www.whitehouse.gov/ostp/nstc.

About the Office of Science and Technology Policy

The Office of Science and Technology Policy (OSTP) was established by the National Science and Technology Policy, Organization, and Priorities Act of 1976. OSTP's responsibilities include advising the President in policy formulation and budget development on questions in which science and technology are important elements; articulating the President's science and technology policy and programs; and fostering strong partnerships among Federal, state, and local governments, and the scientific communities in industry and academia. The Director of OSTP also serves as Assistant to the President for Science and Technology and manages the NSTC. More information is available at www.whitehouse.gov/ostp.

About the Subcommittee on the Social and Behavioral Sciences Team

The Subcommittee on the Social and Behavioral Sciences Team (SBST) contributes to the activities of NSTC's Committee on Technology (CoT). SBST's purpose is to coordinate the application of social and behavioral science research to help Federal agencies advance their policy and program goals and better serve the Nation. SBST works to identify opportunities for Federal agencies to leverage social and behavioral science insights to advance the goals of their policies and programs, demonstrate the impact of these applications, and build capacity for applications of social and behavioral science across Federal agencies.

About this Document

This document was developed by the Subcommittee on the Social and Behavioral Sciences Team. The document was published by OSTP.

End Notes for Executive Summary

[1] Daniel Kahneman, "Maps of Bounded Rationality: Psychology for Behavioral Economics," *American Economic Review* 93 (2003): 1449–1475. Richard H. Thaler and Cass R. Sunstein, *Nudge* (Yale, 2008).

[2] Eric P. Bettinger, Bridget Terry Long, Philip Oreopoulos, and Lisa Sanbonmatsu, "The Role of Application Assistance and Information in College Decisions: Results from the H&R Block Fafsa Experiment," *Quarterly Journal of Economics* 127 (2012): 1205–1242.

[3] U.S. Department of Education, "Fiscal Year 2016 Budget Summary and Background Information," (2015), p. 40.

[4] Brigitte C. Madrian and Dennis F. Shea, "The Power of Suggestion: Inertia in 401(k) Participation and Savings Behavior," *Quarterly Journal of Economics* 116 (2001): 1149–1187. Pension Protection Act of 2006, Public Law 109-280, U.S. Statutes at Large 120 (2006): 780–1172.

[5] Shlomo Benartzi and Richard H. Thaler, "Behavioral Economics and the Retirement Savings Crisis," *Science* 339 (2013): 1152–1153.

End Notes

[1] Daniel Kahneman, "Maps of Bounded Rationality: Psychology for Behavioral Economics," *American Economic Review* 93 (2003): 1449–1475. Richard H. Thaler and Cass R. Sunstein, *Nudge* (Yale, 2008).

[2] Eric P. Bettinger, Bridget Terry Long, Philip Oreopoulos, and Lisa Sanbonmatsu, "The Role of Application Assistance and Information in College Decisions: Results from the H&R Block Fafsa Experiment," *Quarterly Journal of Economics* 127 (2012): 1205–1242.

[3] U.S. Department of Education, "Fiscal Year 2016 Budget Summary and Background Information," (2015), p. 40.

[4] Brigitte C. Madrian and Dennis F. Shea, "The Power of Suggestion: Inertia in 401(k) Participation and Savings Behavior," *Quarterly Journal of Economics* 116 (2001): 1149–1187. Pension Protection Act of 2006, Public Law 109-280, U.S. Statutes at Large 120 (2006): 780–1172.

[5] Shlomo Benartzi and Richard H. Thaler, "Behavioral Economics and the Retirement Savings Crisis," Science 339 (2013): 1152–1153 .

[6] Raj Chetty, "Behavioral Economics and Public Policy: A Pragmatic Perspective," *American Economic Review* 105 (2015): 1–33; Eldar Shafir, ed., *The Behavioral Foundations of Public Policy*, (Princeton University Press, 2012); William J. Congdon, Jeffrey R. Kling, and Sendhil Mullainathan, *Policy and Choice: Public Finance through the Lens of Behavioral Economics,* (Brookings Institution, 2011).

[7] Brigitte C. Madrian, "Applying Insights from Behavioral Economics to Policy Design," *Annual Review of Economics* 6 (2014): 663–688.

[8] The idea, for example, of creating a central, Federal group focused on behavioral economics goes back to at least 2004, when a session was organized by Richard Thaler at the 2004 Annual Meeting of the American Economic Association entitled, "Memos to the Council of Behavioral-Economics Advisors." SBST has also drawn inspiration from international governments, most notably the United Kingdom, which have created similar teams. See: www.behaviouralinsights.co.uk/

[9] For more on the HHS efforts, see the Behavioral Interventions to Advance Self-Sufficiency (BIAS) project, at: www.acf.hhs.gov/programs/opre/ research/project/behavioral-interventions-to-advance-self-sufficiency, For more on the USDA efforts, supporting research centers on behavioral economics and nutrition, see: www.ers.usda.gov/topics/food-choices-health/food-consumption-demand/behavioral-economics, For more on the DOL efforts, investigating Behavioral Interventions for Labor Related Programs, see: www.dol.gov/asp/evaluation/currentstudies/7.htm

[10] Unless otherwise noted, all impact estimates reported below are statistically significant at the 5 percent level; all abstracts also report the 95 percent confidence interval on reported impact estimates.

[11] Marianne Bertrand, Sendhil Mullainathan, and Eldar Shafir, "Behavioral Economics and Marketing in Aid of Decision Making Among the Poor," *Journal of Public Policy & Marketing* 25 (2006): 8–23.

[12] Further details on this and other reported projects are provided in Appendix B: Project Abstracts.

[13] See, e.g.: Saurabh Bhargava and Dayanand S. Manoli, "Psychological Frictions and the Incomplete Take-Up of Social Benefits: Evidence from an IRS Field Experiment," *American Economic Review* (forthcoming).

[14] John Beshears, James J. Choi, David Laibson, and Brigitte C. Madrian, "Simplification and Saving," *Journal of Economic Behavior & Organization* 95 (2013): 130–145. Eleanor Putnam-Farr and Jason Riis, "'Yes, I want to enroll.': Yes/No Response Formats Increase Response Rates in Marketing Communications," (working paper, 2015).

[15] See: www.whitehouse.gov/the-press-office/2015/07/13/fact-sheet-white-house-conference-aging

[16] Punam Anand Keller, Bari Harlam, George Loewenstein, and Kevin G. Volpp, "Enhanced Active Choice: A New Method to Motivate Behavior Change," *Journal of Consumer Psychology* 21 (2011): 376–383.

[17] Gabriel D Carroll, James J. Choi, David Laibson, Brigitte C. Madrian, and Andrew Metrick, "Optimal Defaults and Active Decisions," *Quarterly Journal of Economics* 124 (2009): 1639–1674.

[18] Hengchen Dai, Katherine L. Milkman, and Jason Riis, "The Fresh Start Effect: Temporal Landmarks Motivate Aspirational Behavior," *Management Science* 60 (2014): 2563–2582. Daniel Kahneman and Amos Tversky, "Prospect Theory: An Analysis of Decision under Risk," *Econometrica*, 47 (1979): 263–291.

[19] Siegfried Vögele, *Handbook of Direct Mail: The Dialogue Method of Direct Written Sales Communication* (Prentice Hall, 1992).

[20] Claudia Goldin and Lawrence F. Katz, *The Race between Education and Technology*, (Harvard University Press, 2009).

[21] Benjamin L. Castleman and Lindsay C. Page, *Summer Melt: Supporting Low-Income Students Through the Transition to College* (Cambridge, MA: Harvard Education Press, 2014).

[22] Benjamin L. Castleman and Lindsay C. Page, "Summer Nudging: Can Personalized Text Messages and Peer Mentor Outreach Increase College Going Among Low-Income High School Graduates?," *Journal of Economic Behavior & Organization* 115 (2015): 144–160.

[23] FSA and SBST provided technical assistance on message content and complexity for these projects. The trials themselves (and the relevant data collection) were administered exclusively by the stated outside entities.

[24] Dean Karlan, Margaret McConnell, Sendhil Mullainathan, and Jonathan Zinman, "Getting to the Top of Mind: How Reminders Increase Saving," *Management Science* (forthcoming). Ximena Cadena and Antoinette Schoar, "Remembering to Pay? Reminders vs. Financial Incentives for Loan Payments," (NBER Working Paper No. 17020, 2011). Peter Baird, Leigh Reardon, Dan Cullinan, Drew McDermott, and Patrick Landers, "Reminders to Pay: Using Behavioral Economics to Increase Child Support Payments," (OPRE Report 2015-20, 2015).

[25] Saurabh Bhargava and Dayanand S. Manoli, "Psychological Frictions and the Incomplete Take-Up of Social Benefits: Evidence from an IRS Field Experiment," *American Economic*

Review (forthcoming). Raj Chetty and Emmanuel Saez, "Teaching the Tax Code: Earnings Responses to an Experiment with EITC Recipients," *American Economic Journal: Applied Economics* 5 (2013): 1–31. Jeffrey B. Liebman and Erzo F.P. Luttmer, "Would People Behave Differently If They Better Understood Social Security? Evidence From a Field Experiment," *American Economic Journal: Economic Policy* 7 (2015): 275–299.

[26] See: www.whitehouse.gov/blog/2015/03/10/student-aid-bill-rights-enhancing-protections-student-loan-borrowers

[27] See: www.whitehouse.gov/the-press-office/2015/03/10/fact-sheet-student-aid-bill-rights-taking-action-ensure-strong-consumer-

[28] Daniel Kahneman, Jack L. Knetsch, and Richard H. Thaler, "Experimental Tests of the Endowment Effect and the Coase Theorem," *Journal of Political Economy* 98 (1990): 1325–1348. Tanjim Hossain and John A. List, "The Behavioralist Visits the Factory: Increasing Productivity Using Simple Framing Manipulations," *Management Science* 58 (2012): 2151–2167.

[29] Marianne Bertrand, Sendhil Mullainathan, Eldar Shafir, and Jonathan Zinman, "What's Advertising Content Worth? Evidence from a Consumer Credit Marketing Field Experiment," *Quarterly Journal of Economics* 125 (2010): 263–306. Peter M. Gollwitzer, "Implementation Intentions: Strong Effects of Simple Plans," American Psychologist 54 (1999): 493–503 (1999).

[30] Katherine L. Milkman, John Beshears, James J. Choi, David Laibson, and Brigitte C. Madrian, "Using Implementation Intentions Prompts to Enhance Influenza Vaccination Rates," *Proceedings of the National Academy of Sciences* 108 (2011): 10415–10420.

[31] Paul Slovic, John Monahan, and Donald G. MacGregor, "Violence Risk Assessment and Risk Communication: The Effects of Using Actual Cases, Providing Instruction, and Employing Probability Versus Frequency Formats," *Law and Human Behavior* 24 (2000): 271–296.

[32] William W. Thompson, David K. Shay, Eric Weintraub, Lynnette Brammer, Nancy Cox, Larry J. Anderson, and Keiji Fukuda, "Mortality Associated with Influenza and Respiratory Syncytial Virus in the United States," *JAMA* 289 (2003): 179–186. William W. Thompson, David K. Shay, Eric Weintraub, Lynnette Brammer, Carolyn B. Bridges, Nancy J. Cox, and Keiji Fukuda, "Influenza-Associated Hospitalizations in the United States," *JAMA* 292 (2004): 1333–1340. For flu vaccination coverage rates, see: cdc.gov/flu/fluvaxview/coverage-1314estimates.htm

[33] Michael Kremer, Edward Miguel, Sendhil Mullainathan, Clair Null, and Alix Peterson Zwane, "Social Engineering: Evidence from a Suite of Take-up Experiments in Kenya" (unpublished working paper, April 2011).

[34] Nina Mazar and Dan Ariely, "Dishonesty in Everyday Life and Its Policy Implications," *Journal of Public Policy & Marketing* 25 (2006): 117–126. Lisa L. Shu, Nina Mazar, Francesca Gino, Dan Ariely, and Max H. Bazerman, "Signing at the Beginning Makes Ethics Salient and Decreases Dishonest Self-Reports in Comparison to Signing at the End," *Proceedings of the National Academy of Sciences* 109 (2012): 15197–15200. Michael Hallsworth, John A. List, Robert D. Metcalfe, and Ivo Vlaev, "The Behavioralist as Tax Collector: Using Natural Field Experiments to Enhance Tax Compliance," (NBER Working Paper No. 20007, 2014).

[35] Marsha Blumenthal, Charles Christian, and Joel Slemrod, "Do Normative Appeals Affect Tax Compliance? Evidence From A Controlled Experiment In Minnesota," *National Tax Journal* 54 (2001), 125–138. Michael Hallsworth, John A. List, Robert D. Metcalfe, and Ivo Vlaev, "The Behavioralist as Tax Collector: Using Natural Field Experiments to Enhance Tax Compliance," (NBER Working Paper No. 20007, 2014).

[36] For general background on the IFF see: https://72a.gsa.gov/ifffaq.cfm#01

[37] Lisa L. Shu, Nina Mazar, Francesca Gino, Dan Ariely, and Max H. Bazerman, "Signing at the Beginning Makes Ethics Salient and Decreases Dishonest Self-Reports in Comparison to Signing at the End," *Proceedings of the National Academy of Sciences* 109 (2012): 15197–15200.

[38] Michael Hallsworth, John A. List, Robert D. Metcalfe, and Ivo Vlaev, "The Behavioralist as Tax Collector: Using Natural Field Experiments to Enhance Tax Compliance," (NBER Working Paper No. 20007, 2014). "91 percent of Americans..." calculated based on data available at: newyorkfed.org/ householdcredit/2013-Q1/data/xls/HHD_C_Report_2013Q1.xlsx

[39] Hunt Al lcott, "Social Norms and Energy Conservation," *Journal of Public Economics* 95 (2011): 1082–1095.

[40] Todd Rogers, Katherine L. Milkman, Leslie K. John, and Michael I. Norton, "Making the Best Laid Plans Better: How Plan-Making Increases Follow-Through, *Behavioral Science and Policy* (forthcoming).

[41] For general background information on TSP, see: tsp.gov

[42] Enrollment rates for TSP as of late 2014 are reported here: frtib.gov/pdf/minutes/MM-2014Dec-Att1.pdf The differing enrollment procedures are described at: tsp.gov/planparticipation/eligibility/establishingAccount.shtml

[43] Katherine L. Milkman collaborated with SBST on this project.

[44] John Beshears, James J. Choi, David Laibson, and Brigitte C. Madrian, "Simplification and Saving," *Journal of Economic Behavior & Organization* 95 (2013): 130–145. Eleanor Putnam-Farr and Jason Riis, "'Yes, I want to enroll.': Yes/No Response Formats Increase Response Rates in Marketing Communications," (working paper, 2015).

[45] See: www.whitehouse.gov/the-press-office/2015/07/13/fact-sheet-white-house-conference-aging

[46] Hengchen Dai, Katherine L. Milkman, and Jason Riis, "The Fresh Start Effect: Temporal Landmarks Motivate Aspirational Behavior," *Management Science* 60 (2014): 2563–2582. Daniel Kahneman and Amos Tversky, "Prospect Theory: An Analysis of Decision under Risk," *Econometrica*, 47 (1979): 263–291.

[47] Benjamin L. Castleman and Lindsay C. Page, *Summer Melt: Supporting Low-Income Students Through the Transition to College*, (Cambridge, MA: Harvard Education Press, 2014).

[48] Benjamin L. Castleman and Lindsay C. Page were the lead researchers on this project. FSA and SBST provided technical expertise on message content. The trials themselves (and the relevant data collection) were administered exclusively by the stated outside entities.

[49] Benjamin L. Castleman and Lindsay C. Page, "Summer Nudging: Can Personalized Text Messages and Peer Mentor Outreach Increase College Going Among Low-Income High School Graduates?," *Journal of Economic Behavior & Organization* 115 (2015): 144–160.

[50] See: studentaid.ed.gov/sa/repay-loans/default

[51] Dean Karlan, Margaret McConnell, Sendhil Mullainathan, and Jonathan Zinman, "Getting to the Top of Mind: How Reminders Increase Saving," *Management Science* (forthcoming). Ximena Cadena and Antoinette Schoar, "Remembering to Pay? Reminders vs. Financial Incentives for Loan Payments," (NBER Working Paper No. 17020, 2011). Peter Baird, Leigh Reardon, Dan Cullinan, Drew McDermott, and Patrick Landers, "Reminders to Pay: Using Behavioral Economics to Increase Child Support Payments," (OPRE Report 2015-20, 2015).

[52] See: newyorkfed.org/studentloandebt/

[53] For more on IDR plans, see: studentaid.ed.gov/sa/repay-loans/understand/plans/income-driven

[54] Saurabh Bhargava and Dayanand S. Manoli, "Psychological Frictions and the Incomplete Take-Up of Social Benefits: Evidence from an IRS Field Experiment," *American Economic Review* (forthcoming). Raj Chetty and Emmanuel Saez," Teaching the Tax Code: Earnings Responses to an Experiment with EITC Recipients," *American Economic Journal: Applied Economics 5* (2013): 1–31. Jeffrey B. Liebman and Erzo F.P. Luttmer, "Would People Behave Differently If They Better Understood Social Security? Evidence From a Field Experiment," *American Economic Journal: Economic Policy 7* (2015): 275–299. Daniel Kahneman and Amos Tversky, "Prospect Theory: An Analysis of Decision Under Risk," *Econometrica 47* (1979): 263–291.

[55] See: va.gov/op3/docs/strategicplanning/va2014-2020strategicplan.pdf.

[56] For more on Chapter 36 benefits, see: benefits.va.gov/vocrehab/edu_voc_counseling.asp

[57] David W. Nickerson collaborated with SBST on this project.

[58] The random assignment was stratified by branch of service, state of residence, age, years since discharge, and prior benefits used; to improve statistical efficiency, all analysis includes a dummy variable to account for strata of randomization.

[59] Daniel Kahneman, Jack L. Knetsch, and Richard H. Thaler, "Experimental Tests of the Endowment Effect and the Coase Theorem," *Journal of Political Economy* 98 (1990): 1325–1348. Tanjim Hossain and John A. List, "The Behavioralist Visits the Factory: Increasing Productivity Using Simple Framing Manipulations," *Management Science* 58 (2012): 2151–2167.

[60] USDA News Release 0010.13. http://www.fsa.usda.gov/FSA/printapp?fileName=nr_20130115_rel_0010.html&newsType=newsrel * Dean Karlan collaborated with SBST on this project.

[61] For more information on the FHIM, including the Open Enrollment Period, see www.healthcare.gov.

[62] Katherine L. Milkman, John Beshears, James J. Choi, David Laibson, and Brigitte C. Madrian, "Using Implementation Intentions Prompts to Enhance Influenza Vaccination Rates," *Proceedings of the National Academy of Sciences* 108 (2011): 10415–10420. Marianne Bertrand, Sendhil Mullainathan, Eldar Shafir, and Jonathan Zinman, "What's Advertising Content Worth? Evidence from a Consumer Credit Marketing Field Experiment," *Quarterly Journal of Economics* 125 (2010): 263–306. Hunt Allcott, "Social Norms and Energy Conservation," Journal of Public Economics 95 (2011): 1082–1095. Daniel Kahneman and Amos Tversky, "Prospect Theory: An Analysis of Decision Under Risk," *Econometrica* 47 (1979): 263–291.

[63] Multiple Award Schedule contracts are subject to the IFF. For general background information on the IFF, see: https://72a.gsa.gov/ ifffaq.cfm#01

[64] Lisa L. Shu, Nina Mazar, Francesca Gino, Dan Ariely, and Max H. Bazerman, "Signing at the Beginning Makes Ethics Salient and Decreases Dishonest Self-Reports in Comparison to Signing at the End," *Proceedings of the National Academy of Sciences* 109 (2012): 15197–15200.

[65] For more information, see: fiscal.treasury.gov/fsservices/gov/debtColl/dms/xservg/ debt_crosserv.htm

[66] In practice, agencies have varying policies to determine referral, so age of debt (and other factors) at first receipt by DMS is not uniform across agencies.

[67] Michael Hallsworth, John A. List, Robert D. Metcalfe, and Ivo Vlaev, "The Behavioralist as Tax Collector: Using Natural Field Experiments to Enhance Tax Compliance," (NBER Working Paper No. 20007, 2014).

"91 percent of Americans,,," calculated based on data available here: newyorkfed.org/householdcredit/2013-Q1/data/xls/HHD_C_ Report_2013Q1.xlsx

[68] For a full report, see: Adam Sacarny, David Yokum, Amy Finkelstein, and Shantanu Agrawal, "Reducing Inappropriate Prescribing of Controlled Substances in Medicare Part D: Evidence from a Randomized Intervention," (submitted, 2015).

[69] Department of Health and Human Services, Office of Inspector General, "Retail Pharmacies With Questionable Part D Billing," (OEI-02-09-00600, 2012). Mark Olfson, Marissa King, and Michael Schoenbaum, "Benzodiazepine use in the United States," *JAMA Psychiatry* 72 (2015): 136–142. Government Accountability Office, "Antipsychotic Drug Use: HHS Has Initiatives to Reduce Use among Older Adults in Nursing Homes, but Should Expand Efforts to Other Settings," (GAO-15-211, 2015).

[70] Michael Hallsworth, John A. List, Robert D. Metcalfe, and Ivo Vlaev, "The Behavioralist as Tax Collector: Using Natural Field Experiments to Enhance Tax Compliance," (NBER Working Paper No. 20007, 2014).

[71] Catarina I. Kiefe, Jeroan J. Allison, O. Dale Williams, Sharina D. Person, Michael T. Weaver, and Norman W. Weissman, "Improving Quality Improvement Using Achievable Benchmarks for Physician Feedback: A Randomized Controlled Trial," *JAMA* 285 (2001): 2871–2879.

[72] For more information on the LTD program, see: treasurydirect.gov/indiv/myaccount/myaccount_legacytd.htm

[73] Todd Rogers, Katherine L. Milkman, Leslie K. John, and Michael I. Norton, "Making the Best Laid Plans Better: How Plan-Making Increases Follow-Through, *Behavioral Science and Policy* (forthcoming).

[74] From a 2009 survey conducted by Lexmark, summarized here: govexec.com/pdfs/051209rb1.pdf

[75] Figures on Federal employment taken from: opm.gov/policy-data-oversight/data-analysis-documentation/federal-employmentreports/historical-tables/total-government-employment-since-1962/

[76] Marianne Bertrand, Sendhil Mullainathan, and Eldar Shafir, "A Behavioral-EconomicsView of Poverty," *American Economic Review* 94 (2004): 419–423. Kurt Lewin, *Field Theory in Social Science,* (New York: Harper, 1951).

[77] Background information on the Public Buildings Service is available here: gsa.gov/portal/content/104444

[78] Todd Rogers, Katherine L. Milkman, Leslie K. John, and Michael I. Norton, "Making the Best Laid Plans Better: How Plan-Making Increases Follow-Through, *Behavioral Science and Policy* (forthcoming).

[79] Background information on the Public Buildings Service is available here: gsa.gov/portal/content/104444

[80] Background information on the Public Buildings Service is available here: gsa.gov/portal/content/104444

In: Social and Behavioral Science ...
Editor: Erika Stephans
ISBN: 978-1-63484-293-8

Chapter 2

THE POWER OF PROMPTS: USING BEHAVIORAL INSIGHTS TO ENCOURAGE PEOPLE TO PARTICIPATE*

Nadine Dechausay, Caitlin Anzelone and Leigh Reardon

OVERVIEW

This report presents findings from two behavioral interventions designed to increase the number of participants who attended an informational meeting about a program they enrolled in called the Paycheck Plus Demonstration. The tests are part of the Behavioral Interventions to Advance Self-Sufficiency (BIAS) project, which is the first major opportunity to use a behavioral economics lens to examine programs that serve poor and vulnerable people in the United States.

The first round of experimentation lasted one month. The meetings were offered in person at several locations throughout New York City. The BIAS team designed two kinds of postcards to invite participants to attend these meetings — one that incorporated concepts from behavioral economics (the "behavioral" version), and one that did not (the "standard" version). Half of the sample was sent behavioral postcards and

* This is an edited, reformatted and augmented version of OPRE Report 2015-75, issued by the Office of Planning, Research and Evaluation, Administration for Children and Families, U.S. Department of Health and Human Services, August 2015.

the other half was sent standard postcards. In addition, half of the people within each of these groups were also sent four text message reminders. The messages within the texts were either behavioral or standard, depending on the type of postcards the participant were sent. The study found that:

- Behavioral messaging led to a statistically significant increase of 7 percentage points (or 38 percent) in meeting attendance, compared with standard messaging.
- Sending text messages with postcards produced a statistically significant impact of 5 percentage points (or 26 percent), compared with sending only postcards.
- The highest intensity outreach (behavioral postcards together with behavioral texts) improved meeting attendance by 12 percentage points (or 73 percent), when compared with the lightest-touch approach (only standard postcards).

Behavioral messaging led to a significant and quite large increase in the percentage of participants who attended the meeting. However, the overall number of participants who responded to any outreach effort was still lower than the program operators desired. In an attempt to build on the initial response, a second round of outreach was launched immediately. Participants who did not attend a meeting during Round 1 were randomly assigned to attend either a meeting by phone or a meeting in person. *All participants in Round 2* received communications that were designed using behavioral concepts. The study found that:

- Participants in the phone group responded to the marketing materials more quickly than those in the in-person group, but this effect diminished as the deadline approached.
- In the end, there was no statistically significant difference in response rates between the phone and in-person research groups.

These behavioral experiments reinforce previous findings about the power of behavioral techniques to help people to follow through on an action. At the same time, they demonstrate the challenge of engaging a low-income, urban population in a supplemental informational meeting, even when offered by phone.

Executive Summary

The Behavioral Interventions to Advance Self-Sufficiency (BIAS) project is the first major opportunity to use a behavioral economics lens to examine programs that serve poor and vulnerable people in the United States. Sponsored by the Office of Planning, Research and Evaluation of the Administration for Children and Families in the U.S. Department of Health and Human Services and led by MDRC, the project applies behavioral insights to issues related to the operations, implementation, and efficacy of social service programs and policies. The goal is to learn how tools from behavioral science can be used to deliver programs more effectively and, ultimately, to improve the well-being of low-income children, adults, and families.

This report presents findings from behavioral interventions designed to increase the number of participants who attended an informational meeting about a program they enrolled in called the Paycheck Plus Demonstration. The Paycheck Plus Demonstration is evaluating whether offering single New Yorkers a generous earnings supplement on top of the existing earned income tax credit (EITC) improves their economic well-being and encourages employment. Eligible participants qualify to receive up to $2,000 a year for three years if they work, earn wages within an income cap, and file taxes. Enrollment into the program took place in late 2013 and early 2014. Since participants enrolled about a year before they could receive their first bonus payment (in the spring of 2015), Paycheck Plus program operators invited them to a meeting to remind them of the program's benefits, review its participation requirements, and encourage them to find work or to continue working if they were already employed. The meeting was optional and there was a $50 incentive to encourage attendance.

Program operators anticipated that many participants would not attend the meeting, even when they explained the purpose and offered a monetary incentive. The central question for this BIAS intervention is whether behavioral techniques can be used to increase the attendance rate. Using a process called behavioral diagnosis and design, the team collected quantitative and qualitative data about the EITC and Paycheck Plus programs, and spoke to participants, administrators, and experts. To identify areas where bottlenecks may have occurred, the BIAS team mapped the steps participants needed to take to complete a meeting and hypothesized behavioral reasons for not attending.

The first round of experimentation started in March 2014 and lasted one month. The BIAS team designed two types of postcards: one meant to reflect a typical message that program operators would have produced in the absence of a BIAS intervention (the "standard" version), and one that incorporated concepts from behavioral economics (defined in Appendix Table A.1), including implementation prompting, loss aversion, and prominent deadlines (the "behavioral" version). Additionally, half of the participants were sent text messages. The study contained four research groups. Group 1 was sent only behavioral postcards, and Group 2 was sent behavioral postcards and behavioral text messages. Group 3 was sent only standard postcards, and Group 4 was sent standard postcards and standard text messages.

Figure ES.1 shows the overall effect of using any type of behavioral messaging (Group 1 and Group 2), compared with using any type of standard messaging (Group 3 and Group 4). Behavioral messaging led to a 7 percentage point increase in meeting attendance (over a base of 18.5 percent), compared with standard messaging.

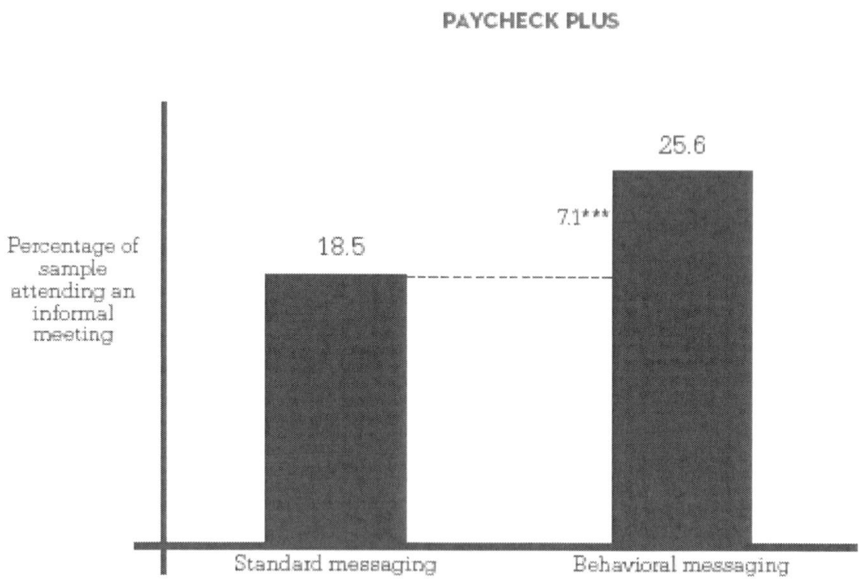

Note: Statistical significance levels are indicated as: * = 10 percent; ** = 5 percent; and *** = 1 percent.

Figure ES.1. Impact of behavioral messaging, round 1.

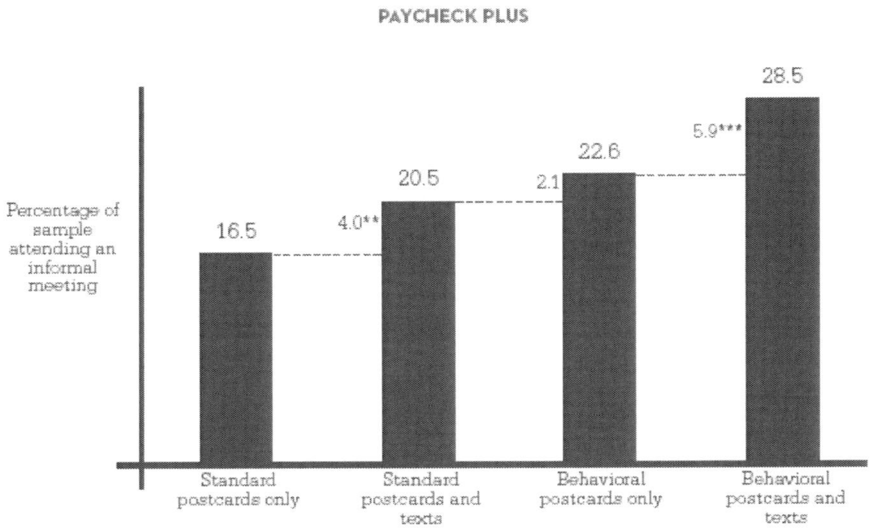

Note: Statistical significance levels are indicated as: * = 10 percent; ** = 5 percent; and *** = 1 percent.

Figure ES.2. Impacts by research group, round 1.

Figure ES.2 presents a further breakdown by each research group. The strongest outcomes were found for the group that was sent *both* behavioral postcards and behavioral text messages. Employing the highest-intensity outreach — sending both behavioral postcards and behavioral texts — resulted in 28.5 percent of the Group 2 sample participating, compared with 16.5 percent who participated in the postcards-only group. As a result, the highest intensity outreach improved response by 12 percentage points (or 73 percent), when compared with the lightest touch, sending only standard postcards. Figure ES.2 also shows that sending text messages with postcards produced statistically significant impacts, compared with sending only postcards, regardless of the type of messaging.

Behavioral messaging led to a large, statistically significant increase in the percentage of participants who attended the meeting. Yet, the overall number of participants who responded to any outreach was still lower than the program operators desired, so the BIAS team immediately launched a second round of outreach to those who did not respond to the first.

Based on a review of findings and feedback from a limited number of participants, the team proposed an intervention that aimed to significantly reduce hassle factors associated with in-person meeting participation by offering a phone conversation instead.

Participants who did not attend a meeting during Round 1 were randomly assigned to one of two conditions: (1) meeting by phone, or (2) meeting in person. In light of the effectiveness of the behavioral principles used in Round 1, *all participants in Round 2* received communications that were designed using behavioral concepts. This round included several different forms of outreach using all communication channels for which the participant had provided contact information and consent — mail, e-mail, text, and robocalls.

The second round of experimentation started in May 2014 and lasted six weeks. The findings showed that:

- Launching a second round of outreach increased the total number of participants who attended a meeting; 655 participants responded to marketing in Round 1 and an additional 832 participants responded to marketing in Round 2.
- Participants in the phone group responded to the marketing materials more quickly than those in the in-person group, but this effect diminished as the deadline approached.
- In the end, there was no statistically significant difference in response rates between the phone and in-person research groups.

These behavioral experiments reinforce previous findings about the power of behavioral techniques, such as implementation prompts, multiple reminders, and highly publicized deadlines, in helping people to follow through on an action. At the same time, they demonstrate the challenge of engaging a low-income, urban population in supplemental informational meetings, even when offered by phone.

THE POWER OF PROMPTS

Using Behavioral Insights to Encourage People to Participate

The Behavioral Interventions to Advance Self-Sufficiency (BIAS) project, sponsored by the Office of Planning, Research and Evaluation of the Administration for Children and Families in the U.S. Department of Health and Human Services, is the first major opportunity to use a behavioral economics lens to look at programs that serve poor and vulnerable people in the United States. Led by MDRC, the project applies behavioral insights to issues related to the operations, implementation, structure, and efficacy of selected social service programs and policies, with the goal of learning how tools from behavioral science can be used to deliver programs more effectively and, ultimately, to improve the wellbeing of low-income children, adults, and families.

This report presents findings from behavioral interventions designed to increase the number of participants who attended an informational meeting about a program they had enrolled in called the Paycheck Plus Demonstration. The Paycheck Plus Demonstration is evaluating a new earned income tax credit (EITC)-like earnings supplement for low-income single adults without dependent children. By increasing the financial returns from work, Paycheck Plus aims to increase employment and reduce poverty. However, like all financial incentive programs, Paycheck Plus relies on participants having a clear understanding of the actions they must take to qualify for the incentive, and the mechanism for claiming it. The informational meeting was designed to ensure that they had this information.

The BIAS team created multiple sets of marketing materials that encouraged participants to attend the meeting, and tested their effectiveness using an experimental design. The central question of this study is whether behavioral techniques can be used to measurably increase engagement with a supplemental component of the Paycheck Plus intervention. To answer this question, the BIAS team launched two successive rounds of tests in a short period. As a result, this study also illustrates some operational lessons from rapid-cycle evaluation. The findings from this study are applicable to programs that anticipate or experience challenges getting participants to attend events, especially when the tangible benefits of participation are in the future or abstract.

The report begins with a brief overview of the Paycheck Plus Demonstration. It then describes how the research team used a method called "behavioral diagnosis and design" to anticipate reasons people might not attend the informational meeting, and used this information to design low-cost behaviorally informed marketing materials. The remainder of the report presents results from two rounds of experimentation.

The Paycheck Plus Demonstration

The federal EITC is one of the largest antipoverty programs in the United States.[1] The credit supplements the earnings of low-income families with children by as much as $6,200 a year and has been successful at increasing employment among single mothers.[2] However, in comparison with large benefits for families with children, the federal EITC for single tax filers without dependent children was capped at a maximum annual payment of just $503 in 2015. This smaller credit for single tax filers is less effective at increasing employment and reducing poverty within this population.[3]

To assess whether a larger EITC benefit for singles can increase employment and reduce poverty, MDRC is evaluating an EITC-like earnings supplement for low-income workers in New York City who do not have dependent children with funding from the Center for Economic Opportunity and the Robin Hood Foundation.[4] From September 2013 through February 2014, 6,000 low-income individuals were enrolled in the Paycheck Plus Demonstration. Half of the individuals were assigned at random to the program group, which was eligible to receive the supplement; the other half were randomly assigned to the control group. Those eligible for the supplement may qualify to receive up to $2,000 a year in 2015, 2016, and 2017 if they work, earn wages within an income cap, and file taxes.

The Food Bank for New York City (Food Bank), which runs a network of Volunteer Income Tax Assistance (VITA) sites and is the lead implementing agency for the Paycheck Plus Demonstration, recruited the study sample. The goal was to recruit a diverse sample of low-wage workers, targeting groups that typically face the most labor market challenges, including the formerly incarcerated, noncustodial parents with arrears, and individuals with little or no earnings. At the time of enrollment, about 12 percent of the sample reported being noncustodial parents and 18 percent reported having ever been incarcerated. About 71 percent were employed in the year before they enrolled in the study, and nearly half of those who did work earned less than $7,000 during the year. Only 24 percent were working full time at the time of enrollment, and the average weekly earnings among those currently working were only $292.

The Paycheck Plus program operators foresaw several potential challenges related to the participants' understanding and ongoing awareness of the program. Many participants recruited into the sample had been disconnected from the labor market and did not know about the

EITC.[5] The study recruiters had limited time to explain the program at the point of enrollment, so program group members may not have fully understood how to qualify for or claim the supplement in 2015. Even if they entered the program with a good understanding, they might forget about Paycheck Plus in the ensuing year. Since participants had to work in 2014 to claim the supplement in 2015, it was imperative that the supplement was on their minds to potentially influence employment-related decisions.

To address these issues, the program operators created an informational meeting for individuals eligible to receive the supplement — in effect, a one-on-one orientation to the program. Starting in March 2014, program group members were invited to attend the meeting at one of Food Bank's VITA sites. As an incentive to attend, program operators offered participants a $50 American Express gift card. The goal of the short meeting was to ensure participants understood the requirements for earning the supplement in subsequent years, and to introduce them to one of the VITA locations where they could claim it in 2015.[6]

Box 1. Behavioral Economics

Behavioral economics, part of the broader field of behavioral science, is the application of psychological insights to economic models of decision making.[*] Innovative research in this area has shown that human decision making is often imperfect and imprecise. People — clients and program administrators alike — procrastinate, get overwhelmed by choices, and miss important details. As a result, they may not always achieve the goals they set for themselves. Principles from behavioral economics can both shed light on decision making and offer new tools to improve outcomes for program participants.

Research has shown that small changes in the environment can facilitate desired behaviors, that planning and commitment devices can be used to improve self-control, and that default rules can produce positive outcomes even for people who fail to act. Over the past decade, behavioral economics has gained popularity in the private and public sectors. For example, credit card machine vendors for New York City taxi cabs leverage the use of defaults to influence customer choice. Passengers paying for their ride with a credit card are prompted by a screen to enter a tip amount, and have the option to either choose one of three default amounts or to enter an amount of their own.

When the default amounts were increased — for example, changing the options from 15, 20, and 25 percent to 20, 25, and 30 percent — the average tip amount increased.[†] In the public sector, California introduced a Fast Track system to streamline the Medicaid enrollment process. Using common behavioral economics strategies, Fast Track has successfully connected eligible families to vital services by making the process easier and reducing the hassle associated with enrollment.[‡] The BIAS team previously partnered with the Franklin County Ohio Child Support Enforcement Agency to use reminders to increase the collection of child support payments. The BIAS team designed and evaluated a behaviorally informed, low-cost outreach effort and found that it increased the percentage of parents making a child support payment by nearly 3 percentage points, compared with the control group's rate of 48.5 percent.[§]

These examples are some of the recent applications of behavioral economics to human behavior. Behavioral tweaks — or "nudges," as they are frequently called — are often meant to be limited in scope. As the prominent psychologist Daniel Kahneman states, behavioral economics is "characterized by achieving medium-sized gains by nano-sized investments."[||] These types of interventions are not always expected, or intended, to achieve enormous impacts or attain a system overhaul. Instead, they are meant to be responsive to behavioral tendencies and to foster change at relatively low cost and effort. For a more detailed overview of behavioral economics, see *Behavioral Economics and Social Policy: Designing Innovative Solutions for Programs Supported by the Administration for Children and Families*.[#]

[*] For an overview of behavioral science, see Kahneman (2011).
[†] Haggag and Paci (2014).
[‡] Lord (2014).
[§] Baird et al. (2015).
[||] Singal (2013).
[#] Richburg-Hayes et al. (2014).

This report focuses on behavioral interventions designed to encourage participants to attend this informational meeting. Behavioral research has shown that even providing monetary incentives and explaining the benefit of completing a task may not be enough to induce action, and people may still miss out on opportunities that are in their economic self-interest. (See Box 1 for an introduction to behavioral economics.) Thus, the BIAS tests focused on preemptive strategies to increase responses to the offer. These tests, which were embedded into the larger Paycheck Plus Demonstration, focused on the immediate outcome of increasing the number of participants who attended the informational meeting to learn more about the program. Results from the larger Paycheck Plus Demonstration, including participants' take-up of the EITC wage-like supplement, will be covered in future MDRC reports.

THE BEHAVIORAL DIAGNOSIS AND DESIGN PROCESS

The BIAS project uses a process called behavioral diagnosis and design to try to improve program outcomes through the application of behavioral principles.[7] Adopting the perspective of the program's end user (in this case, Paycheck Plus program group members), the team searched for barriers related to each step of the process, and designed behavioral interventions to address many of them.

In the first phase of the process, the problem is *defined* in a neutral, measurable way. In the *diagnosis* phase, the BIAS team collects both qualitative and quantitative data to identify what may be causing the problem. The team uses the data to guide hypotheses about the behavioral reasons for participant outcomes.

During the third, *design* phase, the BIAS team uses theories about why bottlenecks are occurring to generate proposals for interventions based on behavioral research. It is important to have a clear theory of change to avoid creating behavioral interventions arbitrarily based on what has worked in other contexts. Interventions are designed to address issues without adding significantly to the cost of a program, which means relatively simple, inexpensive changes. This design phase is followed by the *test* phase, during which behavioral interventions are evaluated using rigorous scientific methods — ideally, randomized controlled trials.

As Figure 1 shows, the process is often iterative, with insights from one test informing the next. In this case, the first four-week implementation period started in March 2014. The team quickly analyzed data in April, and the second round of experimentation was launched in May 2014. The entire research period lasted four months. The following sections describe this process.

Round 1: Testing Two Different Messages, Delivered by Mail and Text

Define

The first phase in the process is to *define* the problem in terms of the desired outcome, without making presumptions about the cause. The team did not define the problem as "participants will not attend an informational meeting because they do not think attending is important." That problem statement makes an explicit assumption about the reasons for low attendance. Rather, the problem the team pursued was "participants may not attend the informational meeting, even when program operators offer a $50 incentive and explain the purpose." This statement was precise enough to be testable without making presumptions about the cause.

Diagnose

To better understand the factors that might influence participants' decisions and actions, the BIAS team reviewed literature and collected qualitative and quantitative data about the EITC and Paycheck Plus programs.[8] During study recruitment, the team spoke to a small number of Paycheck Plus participants and Food Bank staff. Though these conversations were informal and limited in number, they helped the team understand how the program was explained to program group members during enrollment, as well as the questions that they asked about the program. The team also spoke to experts familiar with the EITC, including researchers involved in other studies to increase EITC take-up rates and senior administrators who had worked directly with low-income populations served at VITA sites.

In order to identify areas where bottlenecks may occur, the BIAS team mapped the steps participants needed to take to successfully complete a meeting. Figure 2 includes the behavioral concepts that the BIAS team hypothesized to be most significant in completing a meeting. The concepts are also boldfaced and described below. Full definitions can be found in Appendix A.

- Participants signed up for the Paycheck Plus Demonstration in late 2013 and early 2014, more than a year before they were eligible to receive their first supplement payment (in the spring of 2015). Thus, the benefits of the future supplement may be abstract, or *psychologically distant*, to participants and therefore attending an information session about the supplement may not be at the front of their minds.[9] Additionally, those who are unemployed (55 percent at baseline) may disregard the notice about the meeting because they doubt that they will qualify for the Paycheck Plus supplement.

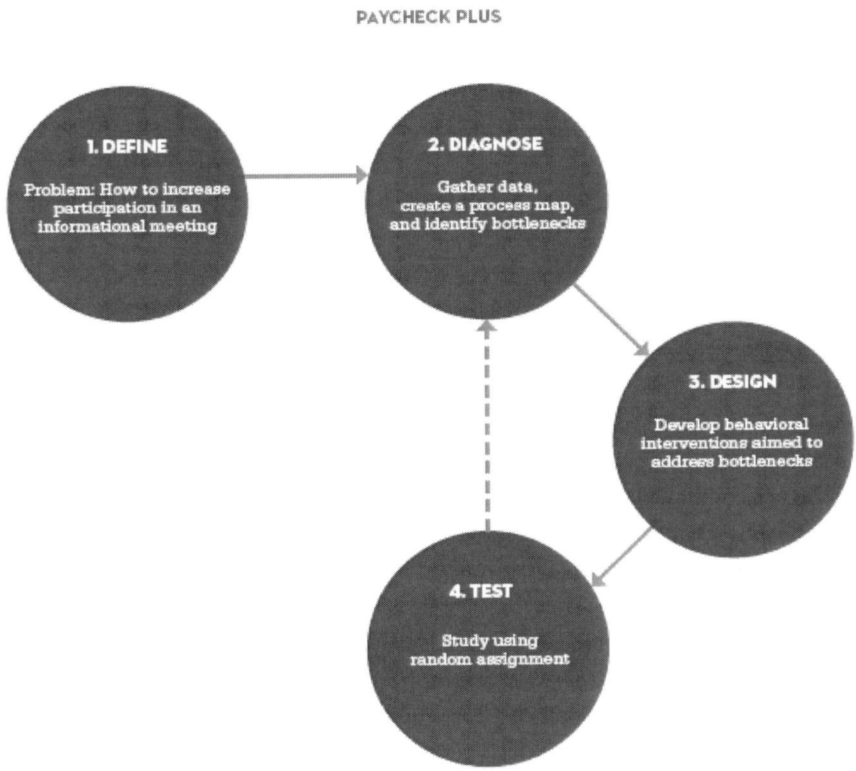

Source: This figure was adapted from a figure created by ideas42.

Note: For a more detailed description of behavioral diagnosis and design, see Richburg-Hayes et al. (2014).

Figure 1. The behavioral diagnosis and design process used in this study.

- *Cognitive scarcity* encompasses the idea that poverty, and the ever-present concerns that come with it, places a heavy burden on people's limited mental resources, and it is likely a factor in the lives of many Paycheck Plus Demonstration participants. For low-income participants who are often juggling personal, financial, health, and other life challenges, they simply may not be able to expend the mental resources needed to plan for and attend the meeting.

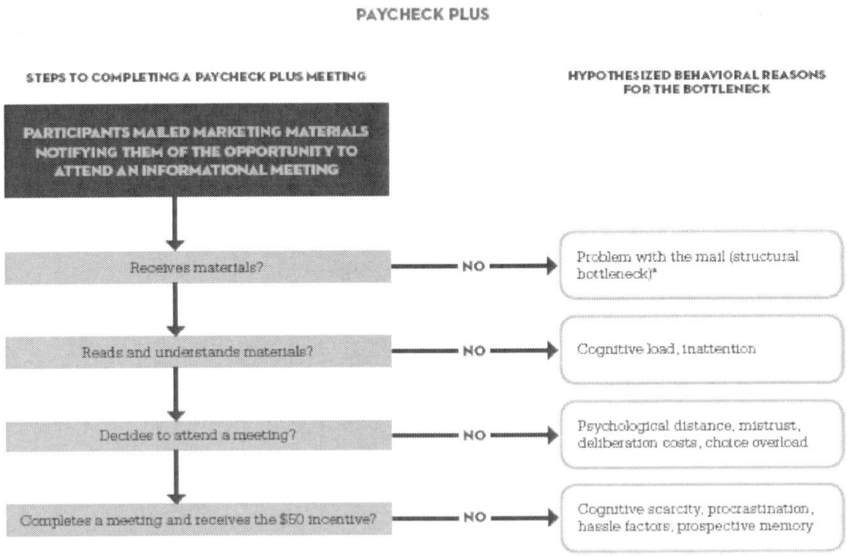

Source: Figure based on MDRC initial fact-finding work with Food Bank and Paycheck Plus staff.

Note: aStructural bottlenecks are not associated with any behavioral concept but are included here for illustrative purposes.

Figure 2. Behavioral map for completing an informational meeting.

- Some participants may be *mistrustful* or skeptical of offers that seem "too good to be true." Receiving a postcard offering a $50 gift card for a short meeting may raise participants' suspicions, especially if they do not recognize the Food Bank logo or Paycheck Plus name.
- Participants may plan to attend the meeting, but *procrastinate* or become distracted by other matters, placing other preferences in front of their plan to attend the meeting.
- Having to show up for a short meeting may not seem like a big hurdle when the reward is valuable information and a generous monetary incentive. But, seemingly insignificant contextual factors can have outsized effects on follow-through, and therefore become *hassle factors*. The travel time or challenges of figuring out how to get to the office may reduce participation.
- Participants may forget their plan or intention to visit a VITA site when the scheduled time comes. This concept is known as *prospective memory* failure.[10]

Table 1. Research Groups, Round 1

Paycheck Plus

RESEARCH GROUP	MESSAGE TYPE	DELIVERY FORMAT	SAMPLE SIZE
1	Behavioral	Two postcards only	740
2	Behavioral	Two postcards and weekly text messages	737
3	Standard	Two postcards only	756
4	Standard	Two postcards and weekly text messages	745

Design

Rather than completely revise the marketing approach that Food Bank used in past outreach campaigns, the intervention used marketing tools — postcards and text messages — already employed by the organization. The BIAS team designed two types of postcards: one meant to reflect a typical message that Food Bank would have produced based on postcards they had distributed in the past (a "standard" version), and one that incorporated concepts from behavioral economics (a "behavioral" version).[11] Both the behavioral and standard postcards contained the critical information that participants needed to successfully attend a meeting, including:

- Summary of the meeting's purpose
- Locations and times of the offered meetings
- Time period to complete the meeting
- Offer of a $50 gift card upon completing the meeting

Paycheck Plus participants who were eligible to receive the supplement in 2015 were randomly assigned into four research groups (as shown in Table 1). All participants were sent postcards, which incorporated either behavioral or standard messaging. In addition, some participants were sent text messages. The language of the text messages was either behavioral (informed by behavioral economics concepts) or standard (similar to the text messages that Food Bank used in prior years).

The following list explains the key behavioral concepts incorporated into the behavioral conditions (Groups 1 and 2) in Round 1. Table 2 demonstrates how these intervention components connect to the hypothesized bottlenecks described earlier, with each intervention component corresponding to a column in the table. Some of the relationships are described below. Figure 3 provides highlights of key behavioral components in the intervention materials.

Table 2. Hypothesized Relationships of Bottlenecks, Behavioral Concepts, and Components of the Intervention

Paycheck Plus

		INTERVENTION COMPONENT						
HYPOTHESIZED BOTTLENECK AND POSSIBLE BEHAVIORAL CONCEPTS	Implementation prompt	Set dead-lines	Simplification	Harness loss aversion	Counter act present bias	Leverage endowed progress effect	Remove hassle factors	Reminders
PARTICIPANT READS AND UNDERSTANDS	MARKETING MATERIALS							
Cognitive load	~		~	~	~	~		
Inattention								~
PARTICIPANT DECIDES TO ATTEND A MEETING								
Psychological distance		V	V	V	V			
Mistrust of the offer	~	~						
Deliberation costs	V		~	~	~	~		
Choice overload			~		~			
PARTICIPANT ATTENDS A MEETING AND RECEIVES THE $50 INCENTIVE								
Cognitive scarcity	~	~	~			~	~	
Procrastination	~	~						
Hassle factors						~	~	
Prospective memory failure								~

NOTES: Behavioral concepts cannot be definitively identified, but rather are hypotheses derived from the behavioral diagnosis and design process that may explain behavioral bottlenecks.

The following are examples of proposed intervention components in the Paycheck Plus study:

Implementation prompt: Encourage participants to make a plan for when they are going to come in for a meeting to close the gap between intention and action.

Set deadlines: Help participants stay on track to meet their goal by eliciting a sense of urgency.

Simplification: Simplify the list of locations where participants may attend the meeting by showing only the two closest to their home address (reduce choice overload, whereby presenting people with a large number of choices hinders decision making).

Harness loss aversion: Use phrases like, "With this postcard, $50 is yours" and "Don't miss out" to make participants feel that the $50 was theirs to lose.

Counteract present bias: Use phrases like, "Only a few days left to claim your $50!" to combat participants weighing that day's concerns more heavily than the goal of making it to an appointment.

Leverage endowed progress effect: Provide participants with a list of "easy steps" that they need to complete, in which the first step is checked off to indicate that they have already started the process toward their goal and completed one of the steps.

Remove hassle factors: Remove steps that hinder participants' ability to complete the action; eliminate the need to physically travel to a location by offering the meeting by phone.

Reminders: Send additional communications as the due date approaches to ensure participants remember to attend.

- An *implementation prompt* encouraged participants to make a *plan* for when they were going to come in for a meeting.[12] ("Check off one location you'll go to; write down when you will go.") The hours of operation were displayed in a graphic to help the reader visualize the week. The standard postcard did not include an implementation prompt and displayed locations and times in a list. As shown in Table 2, implementation prompts aim to address, for example, *cognitive load and deliberation costs.*
- *Deadlines* were prominently displayed. Research has shown that people are more likely to stay on track when deadlines are included.[13] The first behavioral postcard imposed an artificially early deadline of March 29 to prompt immediate action. The second behavioral postcard arrived around March 29, and described the remaining two weeks leading up to the real deadline (April 9) as an extension. The standard postcards did not advertise an early deadline and listed the period that offices were open to participants in neutral language: "Come into a VITA site between March 11 and April 9 to receive a $50 gift card." The deadlines were geared to address the psychology of distance (by providing a concrete period to make the action less abstract), cognitive load, and procrastination.
- The postcard *simplified* the list of office locations where participants could attend the meeting by showing only the two closest to their

home address. This modification aimed to reduce *choice overload*, whereby presenting people with a large number of choices hinders decision making, and make it easier to formulate a travel plan.[14]

- *Loss aversion* was activated and *present bias* leveraged with phrases, such as "With this postcard, $50 is yours," "Don't miss out!" and "Only a few days left to claim your $50!" Present bias is the tendency to weigh current concerns more heavily than future ones, while loss aversion refers to the stronger emotional response that people may have to a loss compared with a gain.[15] More general language was used on the standard postcard, for example, "Receive a $50 gift card." These concepts were employed to make benefits seem more concrete in the current period (limiting psychological distance) and lowering the burden on mental resources by reducing cognitive load.
- The *endowed progress effect,* whereby people are more likely to achieve a goal when they feel they have made progress toward attaining it, was utilized by providing participants with a list of "easy steps" that they needed to take to receive valuable information about Paycheck Plus and the $50 gift card.[16] The first step, "enrolling in Paycheck Plus," was checked off to indicate to participants that they had already started the process and completed one of the steps. Creating a sense of accomplishment was designed to increase their motivation to complete the remaining steps. The standard postcard did not use this technique.

The BIAS team worked with Food Bank to implement the marketing strategy. All groups were mailed the first postcards on March 13 and the second postcards on March 26. Those in the texting conditions were sent one text message per week for four weeks. While the official deadline for attending a meeting was April 9, participants who came in after that date were permitted to attend a meeting through May 6 at the discretion of Food Bank staff.[17]

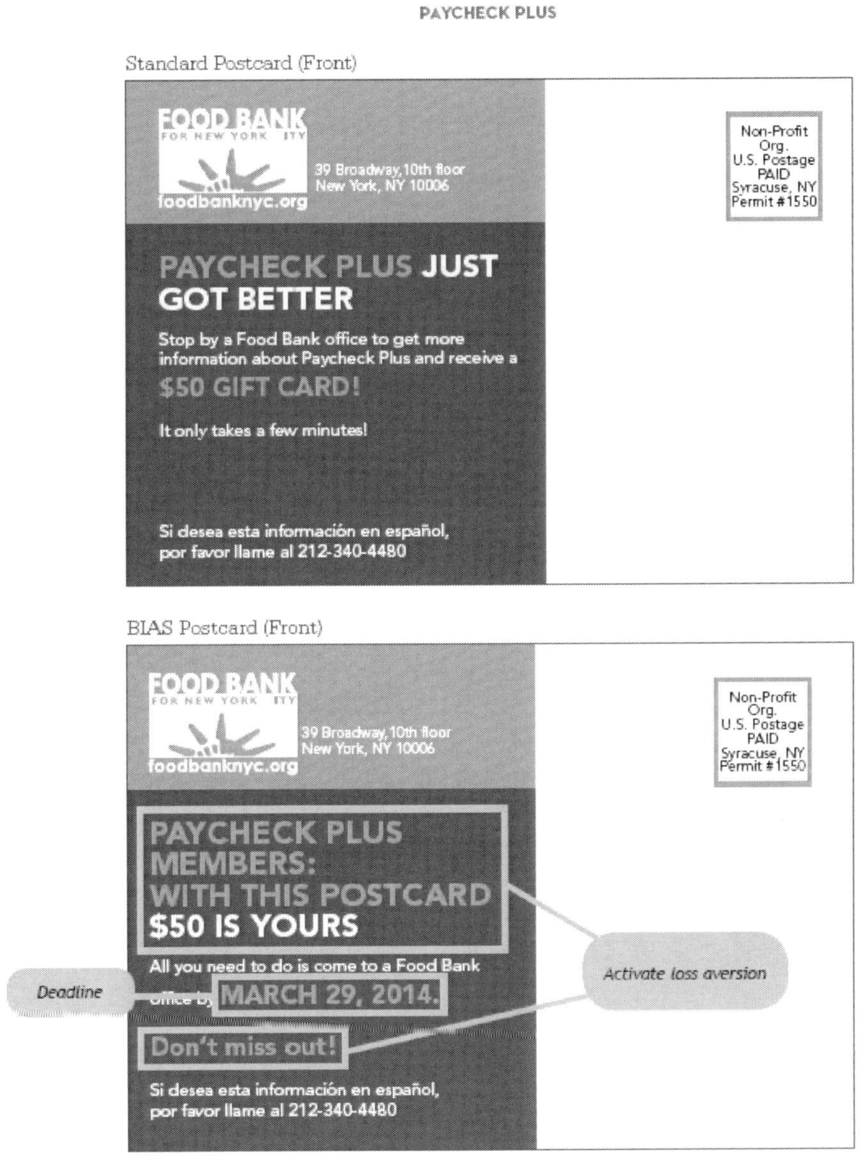

Figure 3. (Continued)

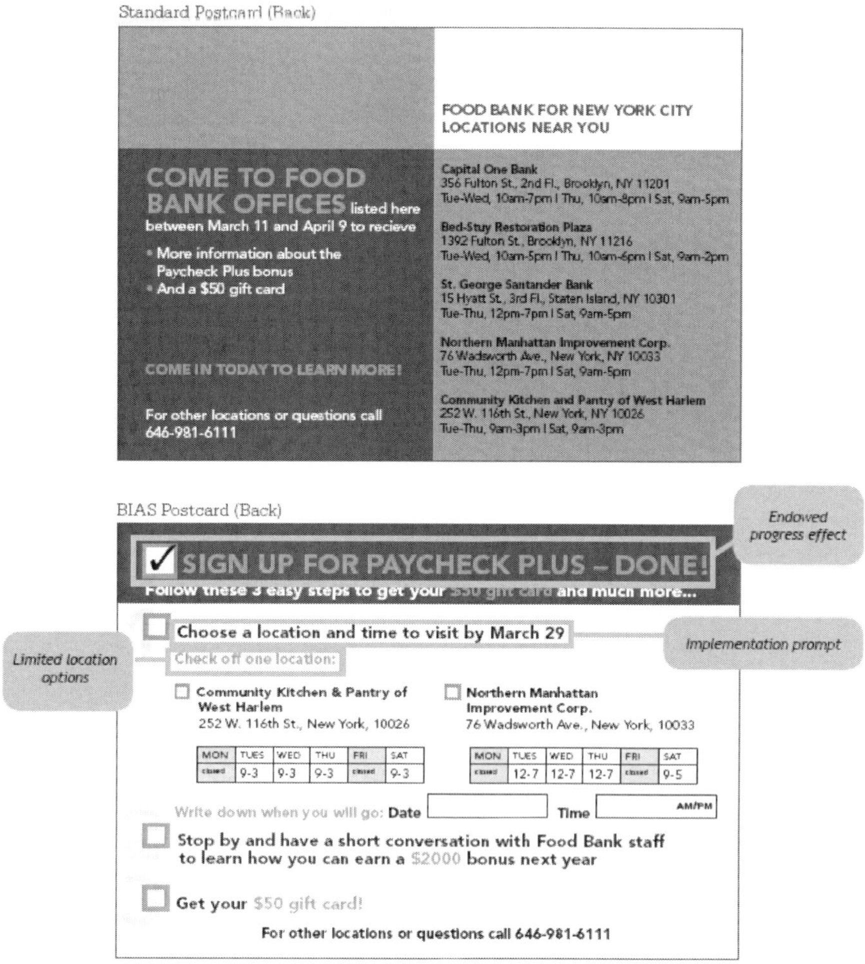

Figure 3. Examples of key behavioral components, round 1.

Test

This study used a factorial design to examine whether behavioral messaging was more effective than standard messaging at getting people to attend the meeting, as well as the marginal impacts of adding text messaging to the marketing campaign.[18] As shown in Table 1, each of the four study groups was assigned to a "message type" — behavioral or standard — and a "delivery format" — postcards only or postcards and text messages. Because the text messages were sent *in addition to* the postcards, Groups 2 and 4 also measured the effect of increasing the number of reminders.[19]

Round 1 Findings

- The intervention was largely implemented as designed, with two challenges.

Figure 4 presents a timeline of when marketing materials were sent to participants. For the first text message, the vendor sent a behavioral and standard text message to both texting groups, rather than sending the appropriate version to each group. This glitch was immediately caught and corrected for all future text messages. In addition, the first set of postcards was mailed on March 13 but did not arrive to the majority of participants until around March 20 to 24. The delay was due to using a nonprofit postage stamp, which was sorted through a different channel from standard mail. As a result, participants had less time to meet the deadline than intended. The second set of postcards was mailed using standard postage and arrived in a more timely manner.

- The behavioral groups appeared to attend meetings more quickly and in higher numbers than the standard groups. The groups that received text messages seemed to respond to the official deadline. This finding can be inferred from the incline of the lines on the survival plot for these groups (Figure 4), which slant more sharply upward around April 8.

Figure 4 displays the attendance rates by research group over time. The figure suggests that all groups increased participation after receiving the second postcard, and that people in the behavioral conditions participated at higher rates compared with those who were sent standard messaging. Those who were sent the behavioral messaging in postcards and texts appeared to respond most quickly to the marketing materials and demonstrated the highest level of participation over time. It also appears that the groups that were sent text messages responded in greater numbers around April 8, when the final text message reminding them of the impending deadline was sent. Although meetings continued to take place up to May 6, participation largely remained flat after the April 9 deadline.

- Behavioral messaging increased meeting participation by 7.1 percentage points, compared with standard messaging. The strongest outcomes were found for the group that was sent both behavioral postcards and texts.

Table 3 shows that 25.6 percent of participants who were sent any behavioral messaging (Groups 1 and 2) attended an informational meeting, compared with 18.5 percent of those who were sent the standard messaging (Groups 3 and 4). Therefore, behavioral messaging increased meeting attendance by 7.1 percentage points (an increase of about 38 percent).

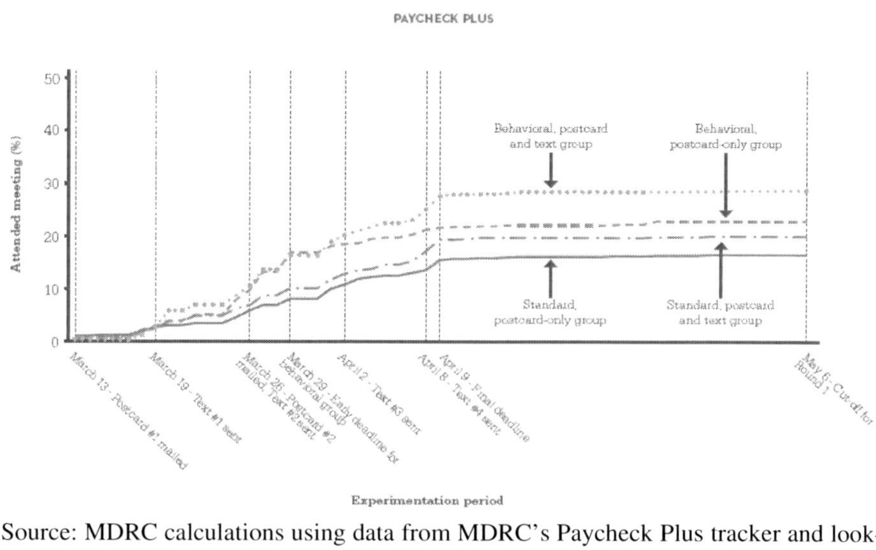

Source: MDRC calculations using data from MDRC's Paycheck Plus tracker and look-up modules, and Food Bank's gift card tracker.

Note: Includes sample members randomly assigned between September 27, 2013, and February 27, 2014.

Figure 4. Percentage of sample members who attended a meeting in round 1, over time, by research group.

Table 3. Impacts on Attending a Paycheck Plus Meeting, by Research Group, Round 1

Paycheck Plus

	HAD MEETING BEFORE ROUND 2 BEGAN		
OUTCOME	SAMPLE SIZE	ADJUSTED MEANS	ESTIMATED DIFFERENCE
Main effect of messaging type (%)			
Behavioral messaging	1,477	25.6	7.1***
Standard messaging	1,501	18.5	
Effect of messaging type by delivery mode (%)			
Behavioral postcards only	740	22.6	6.1***
Standard postcards only	756	16.5	
Behavioral postcards and texts	737	28.5	8.0***
Standard postcards and texts	745	20.5	
Main effect of delivery mode (%)			
Postcards and texts	1,482	24.5	5.0***
Postcards only	1,496	19.5	
Effect of delivery mode by messaging type (%)			
Behavioral postcards and texts	737	28.5	5.9***
Behavioral postcards only	740	22.6	
Standard postcards and texts	745	20.5	4.0**
Standard postcards only	756	16.5	

Source: Calculations using MDRC's Paycheck Plus tracker and look-up module, and Food Bank's gift card tracker.

Notes: There were no statistically significant interaction effects of behavioral messaging and text messages (analysis not shown). That is, the effect of behavioral messaging among individuals who received text messages (effect = 8 percentage points) is not statistically significantly larger than the effect of behavioral messaging among individuals who did not receive text messages (effect = 6.1 percentage points). Similarly, the effect of text messages among individuals who received behavioral messaging (effect = 5.9 percentage points) is not statistically significantly greater than the effect of text messages among individuals who received standard messaging (effect = 4 percentage points). Percentages may not add up due to rounding or missing values.

Among the full sample, 279 individuals (9.4 percent) are missing address information.
Among the sample of groups that received text messages, 336 individuals (22.6 percent) did not provide a cell phone number or agree to be sent a text message.
Estimates were regression-adjusted using ordinary least squares, controlling for pre-random assignment characteristics of sample members. A two-tailed t-test was applied to differences between outcomes for the research groups. Statistical significance levels are indicated as: * = 10 percent; ** = 5 percent; and *** = 1 percent.
The term "messaging" is used to define whether a person received behaviorally informed content, or standard content. The term "delivery mode" is used to define whether a person received only postcards, or postcards and text messages.
April 9 was the deadline communicated to Paycheck Plus participants in postcards and text messages. However, participants who called after April 9, but before May 7 when Round 2 of outreach began, were still able to attend a meeting.

The effect of behavioral messaging was evident regardless of delivery mode. Sample members who were sent only behavioral postcards increased participation by 6.1 percentage points, compared with sample members who were sent only the standard postcards. Behavioral text messages combined with postcards increased participation by 8 percentage points more than those who were sent standard text messages and postcards.

- Sending text messages and postcards increased the response rate by 5 percentage points, compared with sending only postcards.

The bottom section of Table 3 presents the main effect of delivery mode. As the table shows, 24.5 percent of participants (Groups 2 and 4) attended an informational meeting when they were sent both postcards and texts. In contrast, 19.5 percent of participants (Groups 1 and 3) attended when they were sent only postcards. Therefore, sending marketing materials through multiple modes of delivery increased participation by 5 percentage points, or about 26 percent.

The effect of text messages was evident regardless of messaging type. Sending behavioral texts and postcards increased participation by 5.9 percentage points, compared with people who were only sent behavioral postcards (who participated at a rate of 22.6 percent). Sending standard texts and postcards increased participation by 4 percentage points, compared with those who were only sent standard postcards.

- The largest effects were found for people who were sent both behavioral postcards and behavioral texts.

Employing the highest-intensity outreach — sending both behavioral postcards and behavioral texts — resulted in 28.5 percent of people participating, compared with 16.5 percent who participated in the standard postcards-only group. As a result, the highest-intensity outreach improved the response by 12 percentage points (or 73 percent), when compared with the lightest touch, sending only standard postcards.

- Behavioral messaging was more successful with older participants and people who were employed part time or unemployed at baseline. People who were working at baseline were more likely to attend a meeting if they were sent postcards and texts, rather than only postcards. Delivery mode did not make a difference for people who were unemployed at baseline.

Table 4 shows the impact on attending a meeting by subgroup. The BIAS team examined findings for several subgroups based on age, employment status, awareness of the EITC, distance to VITA site, earnings in the past year, and borough of primary residence at the time of study enrollment. Table 4 provides findings for the first two subgroups.[20]

The first set of columns in Table 4 shows that participation rates vary by age and employment status. Older adults were much more likely to respond to the behavioral messaging than the standard messaging, relative to younger sample members. Part-time workers and the unemployed were also more responsive to the behavioral messaging (10.3 and 8.2 percentage points, respectively), relative to those sample members who were employed full time at baseline. No surveys were conducted, so the team can only speculate about why these results were found. Older adults may have been more responsive to the behavioral messaging than younger adults because they were more likely to use the implementation prompts or the messages highlighted in the behavioral messaging about the deadline and be influenced by the financial incentive. People who did not work full time at baseline may have been more responsive to the implementation prompt than those employed full time because it helped them organize their unstructured time and make a plan to attend the meeting. This reasoning assumes that work imposes routines on people's time. Future research should continue to investigate whether people with variable schedules benefit more from implementation prompts and devices for making action plans than people with routines created by their work schedule or other regular commitments.

The second set of columns in the table shows a different pattern of effects for people who were sent texts. Younger participants and those who were working at baseline were more likely to respond to the combination of postcards and text messages. The difference in response rate is 7.1 percentage points for younger adults. This difference, however, cannot be distinguished from the increase in participation of 2.9 percentage points by older adults, which suggests that the delivery mode does not work better for young adults relative to older adults. Full-time and part-time workers were more responsive than those who were unemployed. The texts, which also served as added reminders, seemed to have prompted people who balance work with other responsibilities to remember to go to the meeting.

Round 2: Testing a Change to the Meeting Format

The behavioral messaging conditions clearly increased participants' response to the outreach, but the overall turnout was still lower than the program operators desired. Only 655 out of 2,978 participants, or 22 percent, attended the meeting. Given the relatively simple task and large financial incentive, there seemed to be room to improve this participation rate. Food Bank agreed to hold additional meetings at two of their VITA offices until July.[21] The BIAS team reviewed the findings from Round 1 and rapidly designed another intervention.

Diagnose

During Round 1, the BIAS team visited Food Bank locations and interviewed a small number of Paycheck Plus members who attended their meeting. These conversations, though informal and limited in number, were an opportunity to learn about obstacles that some participants faced.

Table 4. Impacts on Attending a Paycheck Plus Meeting, by Subgroup, Round 1

Paycheck Plus

	Messaging						Delivery Mode			
CHARACTERISTIC	BEHAVIORAL GROUP	STANDARD GROUP	IMPACTS (DIFFERENCE)	P VALUE	DIFFERENCE BETWEEN SUBGROUP IMPACTS[A]	POST-CARDS AND TEXTS	POST-CARDS ONLY	IMPACT (DIFFERENCE)	P VALUE	DIFFERENCE BETWEEN SUBGROUP IMPACTS[A]
Age (%)					†††					
19-34	20.1	16.9	3.2*	0.098		21.9	14.8	7.1***	0.000	
35-64	31.5	20.1	11.4***	0.000		27.3	24.4	2.9	0.192	
Employment status (%)					†					†††
Full time	28.5	28.1	0.4	0.895		33.8	22.5	11.3***	0.001	
Part time	38.3	28.1	10.3***	0.008		37.6	28.6	8.9**	0.019	
Unemployed	19.5	11.3	8.2***	0.000		15.6	15.1	0.5	0.787	

Source: Calculations using MDRC's Paycheck Plus tracker and look-up modules, and Food Bank's gift card tracker.

Notes: Percentages may not add up due to rounding or missing values.

Round 1 meetings are defined for this table as those occurring on or before May 6.

Among the full sample, 279 individuals (9.4 percent) are missing address information.

Among the sample of groups that received text messages, 268 (23.6 percent) did not provide a cell phone number or agree to be sent a text message.

Estimates were regression-adjusted using ordinary least squares, controlling for pre-random assignment characteristics of sample members.

A two-tailed t-test was applied to differences between outcomes for the research groups. Statistical significance levels are indicated as: * = 10 percent; ** = 5 percent; and *** = 1 percent.

The p-value indicates the likelihood that the difference between the research groups arose by chance.

[a]The H-statistic is used to assess whether the difference in impacts between subgroups is statistically significant. Statistical significance levels are indicated as: † = 10 percent;
†† = 5 percent; and ††† = 1 percent.

- The team heard from some participants that they had busy or erratic schedules, and found it challenging to find time to visit the VITA sites during open hours. From these conversations and a review of descriptive statistics of people who showed up for the meeting during Round 1, the team concluded that there were likely *hassle factors* associated with traveling to the Food Bank locations.
- Some participants mentioned receiving a text message but not a postcard. Since postcards are not tracked as undeliverable or returned to the sender if the address is incorrect, there was no way to confirm whether postcards were delivered. Therefore, the BIAS team hypothesized that some participants had *limited information* as a result of not receiving (or reading) the postcard that was mailed.[22]
- *Inattention* may also have led some participants to disregard the communications, perhaps thinking that since they were already part of the Paycheck Plus Demonstration, the meeting might not be relevant to them.

Design

In response to these issues, the team proposed an intervention for participants who did not attend a meeting during Round 1 that aimed to go beyond behavioral changes to the marketing materials and introduce a behavioral change to the *process*. Rather than asking participants to attend the meeting in person, the BIAS team designed a version of the informational meeting that could be delivered over the phone. Participants would receive their gift cards by mail. This approach sought to remove hassle factors associated with traveling to the VITA offices without sacrificing the substance of the meeting.

The Round 1 marketing effort took place between March 13 and May 6. On May 7, the Round 2 BIAS pilot began, targeting participants who did not respond to the first round of postcards, text messages, or both.[23] Participants who did not respond during Round 1 were randomly assigned to one of two conditions:

1) Meeting by phone
2) Meeting in person

To address the concern that participants may not have received the postcards mailed out in Round 1, the team included in this round multiple forms of outreach using all communication channels for which the participant had provided contact information and consent — mail, e-mail, text, and robo-calls.[24] In light of the effectiveness of the behavioral principles used in Round 1, all participants in Round 2 received communications that were designed using behavioral concepts. That is, there was no "standard" condition in this round of experimentation. The marketing strategy incorporated implementation prompting, loss aversion, deadlines, and reducing choice overload (for the reasons stated in the Round 1 "Design" section). Round 2 also incorporated the additional concepts of *personalization* and *social influence* for the following reasons:

- Personalization may help capture participants' attention. Since Round 2 participants may have disregarded or not paid attention to the Round 1 marketing efforts, it was important to try a different strategy to spark their interest.[25] In Round 2, all letters and e-mails began with the person's first name. One e-mail also included the day that the person initially enrolled in the Paycheck Plus Demonstration and an electronic signature of a Paycheck Plus team member.
- Interviews during Round 1 indicated that participants' decisions were strongly influenced by family and friends, which is in line with literature about the role of social influence.[26] Many participants who had filed taxes in the past had chosen the vendor that their family used, or had heard about the Paycheck Plus program through social networks. Social influence was leveraged through phrases such as, "Hundreds of Paycheck Plus members just like you had a short conversation with our staff about how to earn an extra $2,000 next year and got their $50 gift card. Now it's YOUR turn."

Figure 5 provides highlights of key behavioral components in Round 2. The fact that communications to both groups incorporated all these principles reduced the contrast between the in-person and by-phone interventions, and was consistent with the program's operational goal of getting the maximum number of people to attend the informational meeting during the program's short window of opportunity to do outreach. The wording of all communications was identical except for the reference to whether the participant needed to visit an office in person or call the Food Bank hotline. The cost of sending out the communications used in both Round 1 and Round 2 is discussed in Box 2.

Test

The test was designed to determine whether offering the informational meeting by phone increased the percentage of participants who attended a meeting, compared with those who had to attend the meeting in person.

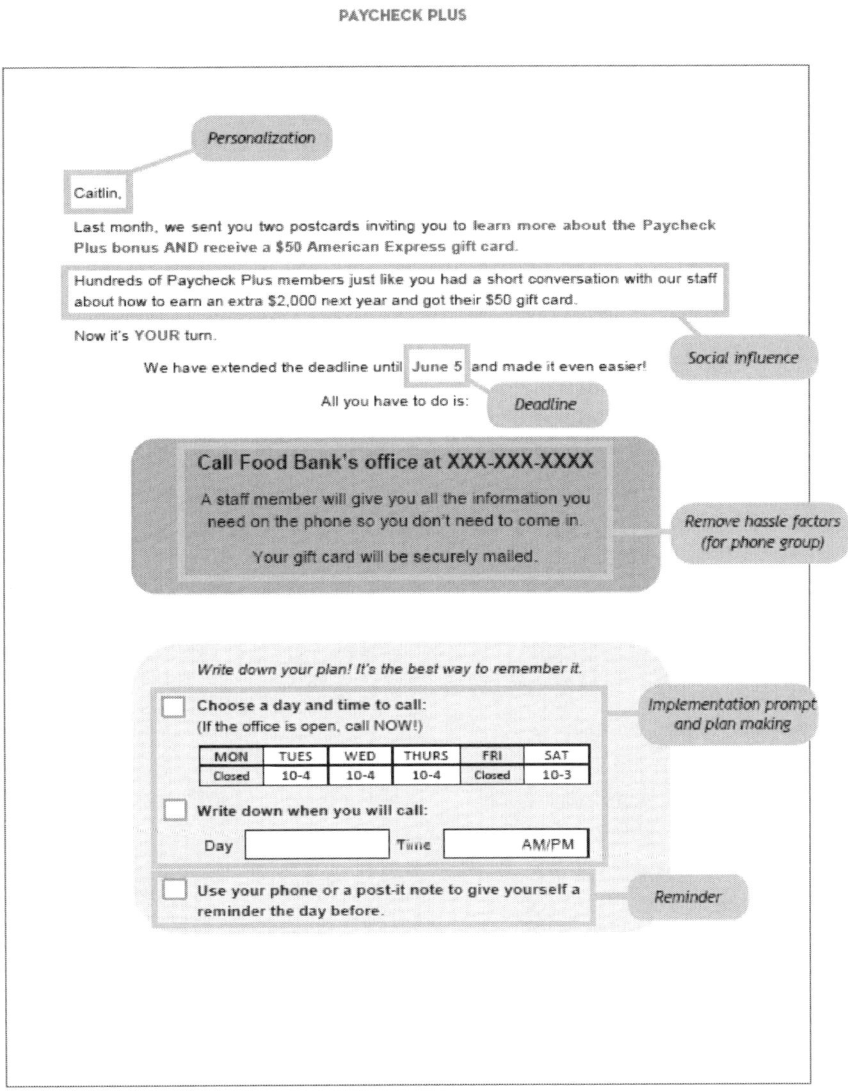

Figure 5. Examples of Key Behavioral Components, Round 2.

Box 2. Cost Considerations

In an effort to inform practice, the costs of this study were calculated for varying levels of effort. The total marketing budget for Round 1 was approximately $5,000. This amount covered the cost of sending two postcards to approximately 2,830 people, and up to four text messages to about 1,100 people, for a total cost of roughly $1.75 per person. A small number of people received only one postcard and fewer text messages because they came in for the meeting before the end of Round 1. The total marketing budget for Round 2 was approximately $3,000, or approximately $1.30 per person, which covered the cost of sending up to two letters, two robocalls, three e-mails, and four text messages to about 2,300 people. As in the earlier round, names were removed from the distribution list weekly as people called or came in for meetings. These base marketing costs would have been lower if letters and postcards had been mailed at the nonprofit postage rate, and if the program operators had the internal capacity to send text messages, rather than needing to use a third-party vendor.

Based on the findings from Round 1, if cost is not a concern, program operators should strongly consider creating behaviorally informed content and sending text messages, given that the combination of those two factors led to the greatest take-up of the informational meeting. However, if resource constraints exist, program operators can still increase response rates over the status quo by sending text messages, which tend to be very inexpensive.

The base marketing costs would increase if programs added some of the following elements that were included in this pilot. However, each of these components is optional.

- *Geocoding*: In this study, participants' home addresses were plotted on a map of New York City and matched to the two closest VITA site locations. This component requires time and access to specialized software to execute it efficiently.
- *Graphic design*: Postcards in Round 1 were designed by a professional graphic designer. In Round 2, the team designed them internally.
- *Personalization*: Letters and e-mails in Round 2 included the participant's first name. This feature was implemented automatically by merging the names with a template, but it required staff time.

Round 2 Findings

- Two implementation challenges occurred. It is not clear how much influence these issues had on the response rate.

First, Food Bank did not have the capacity to answer live calls from participants in the phone group, which was the original intention of the BIAS Round 2 design. Instead, participants in the phone group called Food Bank's hotline, where staff took down their contact information. This list was then regularly forwarded to trained Food Bank staff, who called participants back, usually within three days of the participant's initial call. It was assumed that the hotline could handle all incoming calls; however, interviews with a small sample of participants who did not respond to Round 2 marketing indicate that some members of the phone group called the line and got a busy signal. It is possible that some people who had this experience became discouraged and did not call back. There was no systematic survey of the sample, so the magnitude of this problem cannot be estimated. In addition, some people who called the hotline did not receive a callback from Food Bank staff until after the deadline. To address this issue, the Round 2 test measured both "responded to marketing materials" and "attended a meeting." A small number of participants who called in by the deadline never connected with Food Bank staff to attend a meeting.

Second, the design called for all participants to receive all forms of communication for which they had provided contact information and informed consent. However, due to an internal error, only those assigned to the texting condition in Round 1 were sent text messages in Round 2. As a result of random assignment, there were no differences between groups, meaning that the same proportion of the phone and in-person groups received texts. Despite this error, most participants were sent multiple forms of marketing materials, and almost half were sent seven pieces of marketing materials or more.[27] It is not possible to know what percentage actually read or understood these communications.

- Participants in the phone group responded to the marketing materials more quickly than those in the in-person group, but this effect diminished as the deadline approached.

Figure 6 shows the pattern of meeting participation over time, by research group. It is clear that members of the phone group responded to marketing materials earlier than those in the in-person group and participated at higher levels *until just before the deadline*. Similar to the pattern in Round 1, the impending deadline seemed to trigger a surge in participation for the in-person group. A log-rank test confirms that the difference in participation between the phone and in-person groups was statistically significant from May 7 (the date of the first reminder) to June 2 (the date that the second-to-last e-mail was sent). On June 2, all participants received an e-mail reminder about the impending deadline, as well as text messages over the next two days with a similar message. After June 4, the difference in participation between the two groups was no longer statistically significant.

- In the end, there was no statistically significant difference in response rates between the phone group and the in-person group.

Table 5 shows average response and participation rates for both groups. The first row of the table shows that 37.1 percent of those eligible for phone meetings responded to marketing materials, compared with 34.3 percent of those invited to in-person meetings. This 2.9 percentage point difference is not statistically significant at conventional levels. About the same number of people *completed a meeting in both study groups* because Food Bank staff could not reach 27 people in the phone group who had called the hotline. Almost 10 percent of those in the phone group also opted to go to an office for an in-person meeting (data not presented in the table). These individuals called the hotline as instructed by their outreach materials, but opted to travel to one of the two open VITA locations for the meeting, possibly in order to claim their gift cards immediately.[28]

- Those employed full time at baseline were more responsive to the phone condition than the in-person condition.

Table 6 shows effects by subgroup. Almost half of participants who were employed full time at baseline attended a meeting when given the option to call, compared with 37.3 percent of this group who attended a meeting when asked to come in person. This 10.6 percentage point difference is statistically significant, but because full-time workers cannot be distinguished from part-time workers and unemployed persons in relation to this outcome, this finding cannot be interpreted to mean that the intervention works better for any employment group. Participating in a phone meeting rather than attending one in person may be attractive to people who work full time, but more research should be done to confirm this finding.

DISCUSSION

These behavioral experiments reinforce previous findings about the power of implementation prompts, multiple reminders, and highly publicized deadlines in helping people follow through on a task they choose to complete.[29] In total, the marketing experiments in both rounds led 1,465 people (or 49 percent of the total sample) to attend an optional, informational meeting for the Paycheck Plus program. In Round 1, 655 people attended a meeting. The combined behavioral messaging and text messages in this round led to a 12 percentage point increase in attendance at the informational meeting, compared with the standard postcard alone.

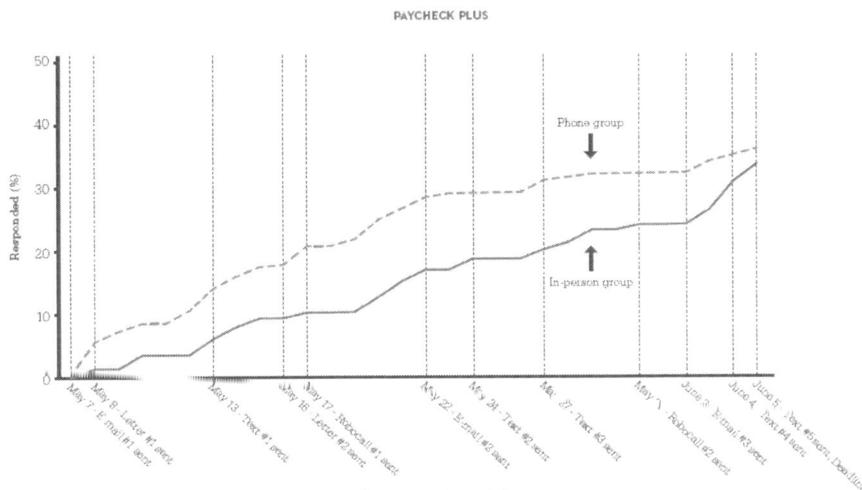

Source: MDRC calculations using data from MDRC's Paycheck Plus tracker and look-up modules, and Food Bank's gift card tracker.

Note: Includes sample members randomly assigned between September 27, 2013, and February 27, 2014.

Figure 6. Percentage of sample members who responded in round 2, over time, by research group.

Table 5. Impacts on Response Rates, by Research Group, Round 2

PAYCHECK PLUS

OUTCOME	PHONE GROUP	IN PERSON GROUP	IMPACT (DIFFE-RENCE)	P VALUE
Responded to marketing material (%)	37.1	34.3	2.9	0.126
Attended Paycheck Plus meetinga (%)	34.8	34.3	0.5	0.807
Sample size	1,162	1,169		

Source: Calculations using data from MDRC's Paycheck Plus tracker and look-up modules, and Food Bank's gift card tracker and call log.

Notes: Percentages may not add up due to rounding or missing values.

Among the Round 2 sample, 271 individuals (11.5 percent) are missing address information and 488 individuals (20.7 percent) are missing a phone number.

Among the sample of groups that received text messages, 268 individuals (23.6 percent) did not provide a cell phone number or agree to be sent a text message.

Estimates were regression-adjusted using ordinary least squares, controlling for pre-random assignment characteristics of sample members.

A two-tailed t-test was applied to differences between outcomes for the research groups. Statistical significance levels are indicated as: * = 10 percent; ** = 5 percent; and *** = 1 percent.

The p-value indicates the likelihood that the difference between the research groups arose by chance.

[a] Round 2 meetings for this table include those that occured between May 7 and June 5 and an additional 103 participants who attended a Paycheck Plus meeting after the June 5 deadline.

In Round 2, 832 participants responded to the marketing, 177 more people than in Round 1. The participants contacted in Round 2 were by definition more difficult to engage than those in Round 1 since they had not responded to earlier outreach. All of them were encouraged to either visit a designated office or call in for the meeting using implementation prompts, reminders, and prominent deadlines. In addition, communications in the second round were personalized, and took advantage of social influence by stating that hundreds of Paycheck Plus members had already responded to this appeal.

One of the central mantras in the application of behavioral science to social programs is that if program operators want people to do something, they should make it easy.[30] The behavioral messaging used in these experiments made the task easier and more salient by helping people develop a plan of action and providing multiple reminders in different formats to help them stick to it. Other research in this field has shown that increasing the number of reminders can improve follow-through, though presumably there is a point at which the return on each additional reminder plateaus.[31]

While the results generally support the notion that making tasks easier increases follow-through, the failure to achieve impacts in Round 2, in which some participants had the option to call in for the meeting, demonstrates the complexity of following this simple rule and the inherent challenges of conducting outreach with a low-income urban population. In the end, approximately the same number of people responded to a significant simplification of the process (converting an in-person meeting to a phone call) as did to changes in the messaging (sending reminders and emphasizing the deadline).[32] There are several possible reasons for this result that may benefit from additional research.

Table 6. Impacts on Response Rates, by Subgroup, Round 2

PAYCHECK PLUS

CHARACTERISTIC	PHONE GROUP	IN PERSON GROUP	IMPACT (DIFFE-RENCE)	DIFFERENCE BETWEEN SUBGROUP P VALUE IMPACTS[a]
Age (%)				
19-34	34.3	32.4	1.9	0.446
35-64	38.8	34.6	4.2	0.135
Employment status (%)				
Full time	47.9	37.3	10.6**	0.016
Part time	49.4	49.2	0.2	0.972
Unemployed	28.5	28.0	0.5	0.847

Source: Calculations using MDRC's data from Paycheck Plus tracker and look-up module, and Food Bank's gift card tracker and call log.

Notes: Percentages may not add up due to rounding or missing values.

Among the Round 2 sample, 271 individuals (11.5 percent) are missing address information and 488 individuals (20.7 percent) are missing a phone number.

Among the sample of groups that received text messages, 268 individuals (23.6 percent) did not provide a cell phone number or agree to be sent a text message.

Estimates were regression-adjusted using ordinary least squares, controlling for pre-random assignment characteristics of sample members.

A two-tailed t-test was applied to differences between outcomes for the research groups. Statistical significance levels are indicated as: * = 10 percent; ** = 5 percent; and *** = 1 percent.
The p-value indicates the likelihood that the difference between the research groups arose by chance.
[a]The H-statistic is used to assess whether the difference in impacts between subgroups is statistically significant. Statistical significance levels are indicated as follows: † = 10 percent; †† = 5 percent; ††† = 1 percent.

First, participants in the phone group may have overestimated the likelihood that they would make the call, since it seemed like such a simple task. As a result, they may not have used the implementation supports in the outreach materials because they did not think they needed them, but then ran out of time to respond. Second, the $50 incentive to attend the meeting may have activated a sense of mistrust for this group in particular. By removing the hassles associated with attending the meeting in person but keeping the same incentive amount, the "ask" (the action required to qualify for the incentive) may have seemed too good to be true. Based on the concept of contextual inference, participants may have assumed that the meeting would be unpleasant and decided that the incentive was not worth the potential discomfort.[33] Future research should test the effect of various incentive amounts on response rates in experiments in which hassle factors have been removed from a task. In addition, it may be useful to test a version of this design that includes some reminders focused entirely on intrinsic reasons to attend the meeting (for instance, to get more information about how to improve one's economic situation).[34] This approach may appeal to some people who are suspicious of or not strongly motivated by a financial incentive.

These experiments demonstrate the challenge of engaging people who live in economically distressed circumstances in supplemental activities. The invitation to participate in these activities runs the risk of being overlooked, misunderstood, or not received at all. When some participants who did not respond to any of the marketing efforts were asked why they had not come in, most said they had not seen or paid enough attention to the materials to understand their purpose. Figures 4 and 6 show that the percentage of participants who responded to the marketing increased as the number of reminders increased, indicating that getting people's attention can be very difficult. The main lesson for program operators is that, rather than trying to reengage participants, they should consider whether or not they can deliver all essential information at a time when participants must be present without overloading them or compromising program efficiency. If not, program operators should consider using behavioral insights to design and develop the content of their outreach materials as much a priority as raising money for financial incentives.

LOOKING FORWARD

In addition to the work in the Paycheck Plus Demonstration, the BIAS project has conducted pilots with other partners, including the Oklahoma Department of Human Services, the Indiana Office of Early Childhood and Out of School Learning, the Cuyahoga (Ohio) Department of Jobs and Family Services, and the Los Angeles County (California) Department of Public Social Services. Results from these pilots will be published as they become available to further inform this burgeoning field.

APPENDIX

Appendix Table A.1. Behavioral Term Definitions

PAYCHECK PLUS

CONCEPT	DEFINITION
Choice overload	The inability to compare choices across meaningful metrics because too many choices have been provided. An excess of choices for people can increase the burden on mental resources and the time and mental energy required to make a choice, reducing the net satisfaction that can be derived from making a decision or even paralyzing some individuals and preventing them from being able to make a decision at all.
Cognitive load	Overburdened mental resources that impair individual decision making. People typically think that they will be able to pay attention to information and then understand and remember it as long as it is important. However, an individual's mental resources, which are often taken for granted, are not unlimited and are more fallible than people often recognize. Challenges and emotional stress can drain these mental resources and actually make it difficult to make good decisions.
Cognitive scarcity	The pressure of negotiating life under conditions of poverty, which exacts a particularly high toll on cognitive resources.
Deadlines	The latest time or date by which something should be completed.
Deliberation costs	The costs — in time or in mental effort — of making a decision.

Appendix Table A.1. (Continued)

CONCEPT	DEFINITION
Endowed progress effect	The phenomenon whereby people provided with artificial advancement toward a goal exhibit greater persistence toward reaching the goal.
Hassle factors	A feature or situational detail that makes a behavior harder to accomplish. This could be, for example, a small barrier to completing a task, such as filling out a form or waiting in line. While these factors may seem trivial and are often neglected in program design, reducing or eliminating them can have an outsized impact on outcomes.
Implementation prompt	Ways to assist people in plan making, or forming implementation intentions, which can facilitate the fulfillment of goals.
Inattention	Lack of attention.
Limited information	Lack of information about an event or process.
Loss aversion	The tendency for decisions and behavior to be influenced by the wish to avoid a loss. When a decision is framed in terms of a loss or a gain, it affects the decision maker's response. When loss aversion is operat-ing, people experience a loss as more painful than when they experience an equivalent gain as pleasurable. For example, when loss aversion is at work, the pain of losing $20 is greater than the pleasure of finding $20. Thus, people's preferences are skewed toward avoiding the loss. When program designers rely on loss aversion to increase the number of drivers who observe the speed limit, for example, they believe that fining noncompliant drivers is more effective than rewarding compliant drivers.
Mistrust	The lack of willingness to place one's resources at the disposal of another party outside of a formal legal framework.
Plan making	Committing to a specific plan for a goal that not only potentially facilitates accomplishing tasks, but also reduces the burden on an individual's mental resources.
Personalization	Techniques designed to make communication less generic.
Present bias	Giving more weight to present concerns than future ones. People tend to make plans to do unpleasant tasks "tomorrow," and make the same choice when "tomorrow" becomes "today."
Procrastination	The practice of carrying out less urgent tasks in preference to more urgent ones, or doing more pleasur - able things in place of less pleasurable ones, and thus putting off impending tasks to a later time, some - times to the "last minute" before the deadline.
Prospective memory	Remembering to perform a planned action or intention at the appropriate time.
Psychological distance	The "distance" (spatial, temporal, or probable) between an individual and some outcome or decision. When an event is psychologically

CONCEPT	DEFINITION
	distant, it is perceived in an abstract manner, and potentially important details are disregarded.
Simplification	To reduce in complexity or make easier to understand.
Social influence	Directly or indirectly fostering a behavior through direct or indirect persuasion. For example, an influential peer or authority figure can often establish the guidelines for socially appropriate and inappropriate behavior.
Trust	The willingness to place one's resources at the disposal of another party outside of a formal legal framework.

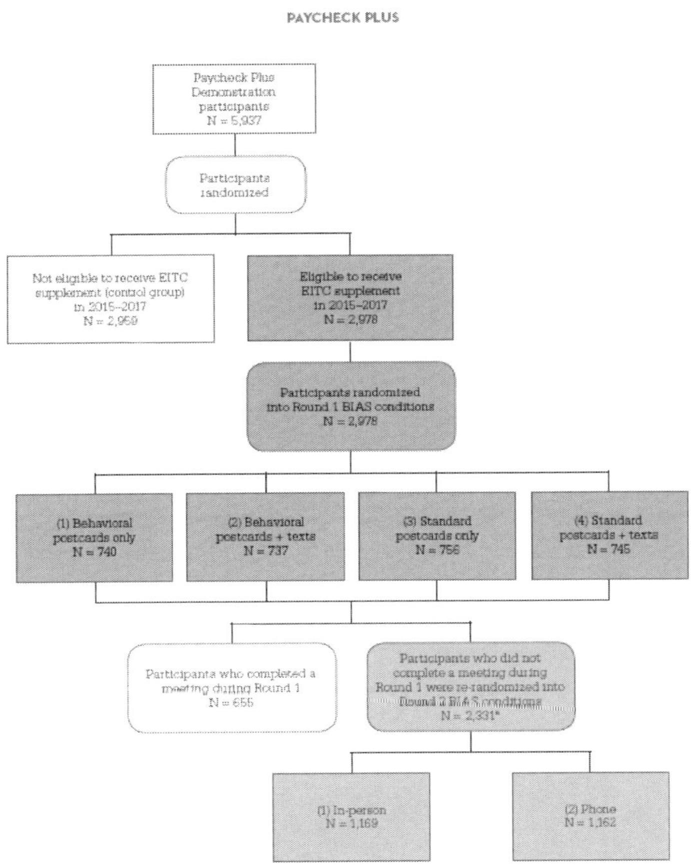

Note:

[a] Eight participants were included in the analysis sample in Round 2 who were not included in the Round 1 sample because their consent forms were obtained later.

Appendix Figure A.1. Embedded bias research design, rounds 1 and 2.

References

Baird, Peter, Leigh Reardon, Dan Cullinan, Drew McDermott, and Patrick Landers. 2015. *Reminders to Pay: Using Behavioral Economics to Increase Child Support Payments*. OPRE Report 2015-20. Washington, DC: Office of Planning, Research and Evaluation, Administration for Children and Families, U.S. Department of Health and Human Services.

Berlin, Gordon L. 2007. "Rewarding the Work of Individuals: A Counterintuitive Approach to Reducing Poverty and Strengthening Families." *The Future of Children* 17, 2: 17-42.

Bhargava, Saurabh, and Dayanand Manoli. 2011. *Why Are Benefits Left on the Table? Assessing the Role of Information, Complexity, and Stigma on Take-up with an IRS Field Experiment*. Austin, TX: University of Texas.

Brandimonte, Maria E., Gilles O. Einstein, and Mark A. McDaniel. 1996. *Prospective Memory: Theory and Applications*. New York: Lawrence Erlbaum Associates Publishers.

Brunnermeier, Markus K., Filippos Papakonstantinou, and Jonathan A. Parker. 2013. "Optimal Time-Inconsistent Beliefs: Misplanning, Procrastination, and Commitment." Working Paper. Princeton, NJ: Princeton University.

Chetty, Raj, John N. Friedman, and Emmanuel Saez. 2012. "Using Differences in Knowledge Across Neighborhoods to Uncover the Impacts of the EITC on Earnings." *American Economic Review* 103, 7: 2683-2721.

Chetty, Raj, and Emmanuel Saez. 2013. "Teaching the Tax Code: Earnings Responses to an Experiment with EITC Recipients." *American Economic Journal: Applied Economics* 5, 1: 1-31.

Dahl, Gordon B., and Lance Lochner. 2012. "The Impact of Family Income on Child Achievement: Evidence from Changes in the Earned Income Tax Credit." *American Economic Review* 102, 5: 1927-1956.

Dismukes, Key. 2006. "Concurrent Task Management and Prospective Memory: Pilot Error as a Model for the Vulnerability of Experts." *Proceedings of the Human Factors and Ergonomics Society Annual Meeting* 50, 9: 909-913.

Edelman, Peter, Harry J. Holzer, and Paul Offner. 2006. *Reconnecting Disadvantaged Young Men*. Washington, DC: Urban Institute.

Eissa, Nada, and Hilary W. Hoynes. 2006. *Behavioral Responses to Taxes: The Earned Income Tax Credit and Labor Supply*. Cambridge, MA: National Bureau of Economic Research.

Eissa, Nada, and Jeffrey B. Liebman. 1996. "Labor Supply Response to the Earned Income Tax Credit." *The Quarterly Journal of Economics* 111, 2: 605-637.

Garner, Randy. 2005. "Post-It Note Persuasion: A Sticky Influence." *Journal of Consumer Psychology* 15, 3: 230-237.

Gollwitzer, Peter M. 1999. "Implementation Intentions: Strong Effects of Simple Plans." *American Psychologist* 54, 7: 493-503.

Greenstein, Robert, and Isaac Shapiro. 1998. *New Research Findings on the Effects of the Earned Income Tax Credit*. Washington, DC: Center on Budget and Policy Priorities.

Haggag, Kareem, and Giovanni Paci. 2014. "Default Tips." *American Economic Journal: Applied Economics* 6, 3: 1-19.

Hochman, Guy, and Eldad Yechiam. 2011. "Loss Aversion in the Eye and in the Heart: The Autonomic Nervous System's Responses to Losses." *Journal of Behavioral Decision Making* 24, 2: 140-156.

Holt, Steve. 2006. *The Earned Income Tax Credit at Age 30: What We Know*. Washington, DC: The Brookings Institution.

Howard, Eboni, Marie-Andree Somers, and James Taylor. 2013. "Methods for Disentangling the Effects of Individual Components of Coaching in Head Start." Presented at the Association for Public Policy Analysis and Management Annual Research Conference, Washington, DC, November 7–9, 2013.

Iyengar, Sheena S., and Mark R. Lepper. 2000. "When Choice Is Demotivating: Can One Desire Too Much of a Good Thing?" *Journal of Personality and Social Psychology* 79, 6: 995-1006.

Janowski, Vanessa, and Antonio Rangel. 2011. "Differences in Loss Aversion Are Partially Driven by Differences in Excess Attention to Losses." Presented at the Annual International Meeting of the Economic Science Association, Chicago, July 7–10, 2011.

Kahneman, Danicl. 2011. *Thinking, Fast and Slow*. New York: Farrar, Straus and Giroux.

Kahneman, Daniel, Jack L. Knetsch, and Richard H. Thaler. 1990. "Experimental Tests of the Endowment Effect and the Coase Theorem." *Journal of Political Economy* 98, 6: 1325-1348.

Kamenica, Emir. 2012. "Behavioral Economics and Psychology of Incentives." *Annual Review of Economics* 4, 1: 427-452. Laibson, David. 1997. "Golden Eggs and Hyperbolic Discounting." *The Quarterly Journal of Economics* 112, 2: 443-478.

Lantz, Paula M., Debra Stencil, MaryAnn T. Lippert, Sarah Beversdorf, Linda Jaros, and Patrick L. Remington. 1995. "Breast and Cervical Cancer Screening in a Low-Income Managed Care Sample: The Efficacy of Physician Letters and Phone Calls." *American Journal of Political Science* 85, 6: 834-836.

Lord, Julianna. 2014. "Fast Track Eases Medicaid Enrollment, but Implementation Matters Too." New America Foundation. Website: http://assets.newamerica.net/blogmain.

Masicampo, E. J., and Roy F. Baumeister. 2011. "Consider It Done! Plan Making Can Eliminate the Cognitive Effects of Unfulfilled Goals." *Psychological Review* 120, 2: 395-410.

Milkman, Katherine L., John Beshears, James Choi, David Laibson, and Brigitte Madrian. 2011. "Using Implementation Intentions Prompts to Enhance Influenza Vaccination Rates." *Proceedings of the National Academy of Sciences* 108, 26: 10415-10420.

Milkman, Katherine L., John Beshears, James Choi, David Laibson, and Brigitte Madrian. 2012. *Following Through on Good Intentions: The Power of Planning Prompts*. Cambridge, MA: National Bureau of Economic Research.

Nichols, Austin, Elaine Sorensen, and Kyle Lippold. 2012. *The New York Noncustodial Parent EITC: Its Impact on Child Support Payments and Employment*. Washington, DC: Urban Institute.

Nickerson, David W., and Todd Rogers. 2010. "Do You Have a Voting Plan?: Implementation Intentions, Voter Turnout, and Organic Plan Making." *Psychological Science* 21, 2: 194-199.

Nunes, Joseph C., and Xavier Dreze. 2006. "The Endowed Progress Effect: How Artificial Advancement Increases Effort." *Journal of Consumer Research* 32, 4: 504-512.

Pardoe, Rachel, and Dan Bloom. 2014. *Paycheck Plus: A New Antipoverty Strategy for Single Adults*. New York, NY: MDRC.

Pronin, Emily, Christopher Olivola, and Kathleen Kennedy. 2008. "Doing Unto Future Selves As You Would Do Unto Others: Psychological Distance and Decision Making." *Personality and Social Psychology Bulletin* 34, 2: 224-236.

Richburg-Hayes, Lashawn, Caitlin Anzelone, Nadine Dechausay, Saugato Datta, Alexandra Fiorillo, Louis Potok, Matthew Darling, and John Balz. 2014. *Behavioral Economics and Social Policy: Designing Innovative Solutions for Programs Supported by the Administration for Children and Families*. OPRE Report 2014-16a. Washington, DC: Office of

Planning, Research and Evaluation, Administration for Children and Families, U.S. Department of Health and Human Services.
Ross, Lee, and Richard E. Nisbett. 1991. *The Person and the Situation: Perspectives of Social Psychology*. Philadelphia: McGraw-Hill.
Ryan, Richard M., Edward L. Deci. 2000. "Extrinsic Motivations: Classic Definitions and New Directions." *Contemporary Educational Psychology* 25, 1: 54-67.
Saez, Emannuel. 2010. "Do Taxpayers Bunch at Kink Points?" *American Economic Journal: Economic Policy* 2, 3: 180-212.
Scholz, John K. 2007. *Employment-Based Tax Credits for Low-Skilled Workers*. Washington, DC: The Brookings Institution.
Service, Owain, Michael Hallsworth, David Halpern, Felicity Algate, Rory Gallagher, Sam Nguyen, Simon Rudd, Michael Sanders, with Marcos Pelenur, Alex Gyani, Hugo Harper, Joanne Reinhard, and Elspeth Kirkman. 2014. "EAST: Four Simple Ways to Apply Behavioural Insights." London: The Behavioural Insights Team.
Singal, Jesse. 2013. "Daniel Kahneman's Gripe With Behavioral Economics." *The Daily Beast* (April 26).
Sunstein, Cass R. 2003. "What's Available? Social Influences and Behavioral Economics." *Northwestern University Law Review* 97: 1295-1314.
Tax Policy Center. 2014. "Taxation and the Family: What is the Earned Income Tax Credit?" *The Tax Policy Briefing Book.* Washington, DC: Tax Policy Center. Website: www.taxpolicycenter.org/briefing-book/ key-elements/family/eitc. cfm.
Touchette, Daniel R., and Nancy L. Shapiro. 2008. "Medication Compliance, Adherence, and Persistence: Current Status of Behavioral and Educational Interventions to Improve Outcomes." *Journal of Managed Care Pharmacy* 14, 6: 2-10.

End Notes

[1] The federal EITC is a tax credit for low-income working people that rewards and encourages work. The amount of EITC depends on a recipient's income, marital status, and number of qualifying children. Workers receive the credit beginning with their first dollar of earned income; the amount of the credit rises with earned income until it reaches a maximum level and then begins to phase out at higher income levels. The EITC is "refundable," which means that if it exceeds a low-wage worker's income tax liability, the Internal Revenue Service will refund the balance (Tax Policy Center, 2014).

[2] Berlin (2007); Edelman, Holzer, and Offner (2006); Scholz (2007), Eissa and Hoynes (2006); Holt (2006); Dahl and Lochner (2012); Greenstein and Shapiro (1998).

[3] Eissa and Hoynes (2006).

[4] Pardoe and Bloom (2014).

[5] Food Bank directed its outreach effort at several channels, including former VITA clients, food pantries and soup kitchens, programs that serve formerly incarcerated people, workforce and job-training organizations, one-stop career centers, community colleges, fatherhood programs, and social service agencies, all places that serve low-income, single adults. Within the Paycheck Plus sample, 46 percent were aware of the EITC at baseline.

[6] Program operators also implemented another study embedded in the Paycheck Plus Demonstration during the informational meeting, which focused on providing an employment referral to a portion of the program group once they showed up at the VITA site. The goal of providing a subset of Paycheck Plus program group members with an employment referral is to determine whether additional assistance in finding employment, in addition to the offer of a bonus, would increase the number of program group members who earn the bonus and the size of those bonuses in 2015. The details of this embedded study will be covered in future MDRC reports.

[7] ideas42, an early partner in the BIAS project, developed a methodology called "behavioral diagnosis and design" for applying insights from behavioral economics to improve program outcomes. The process presented in this document, also called behavioral diagnosis and design, is a version that has been refined for the BIAS project.

[8] Reviewed research includes Bhargava and Manoli (2011); Nichols, Sorensen, and Lippold (2012); Eissa and Hoynes (2006); Eissa and Liebman (1996); Saez (2010); Chetty, Friedman, and Saez (2012); and Chetty and Saez (2013).

[9] Pronin, Olivola, and Kennedy (2008).

[10] Dismukes (2006); Brandimonte, Einstein, and McDaniel (1996).

[11] This BIAS study is unique in that the team created the standard materials in addition to the behavioral materials. In the absence of the behavioral tests, Food Bank and Paycheck Plus program operators would have still developed a marketing campaign to notify participants of the meeting opportunity. As such, the BIAS team worked with Food Bank to develop the standard version so that it would mimic Food Bank's typical strategy, and then worked independently to create the behavioral version. The team reviewed postcards that Food Bank sent to clients during the 2014 tax season to encourage them to complete their taxes at a VITA site. While the postcards developed for this project had a different purpose (to encourage people to come in for an informational meeting, instead of to complete taxes), the standard postcard for this project followed a similar layout and format to the tax postcards. For example, Food Bank's tax postcards list locations by borough, so the standard postcard developed for the informational meeting did the same.

[12] Milkman et al. (2011, 2012); Nickerson and Rogers (2010); Masicampo and Baumeister (2011); and Gollwitzer (1999).

[13] Brunnermeier, Papakonstantinou, and Parker (2013).

[14] Iyengar and Lepper (2000); Kahneman (2011).

[15] Kahneman, Knetsch, and Thaler (1990); Hochman and Yechiam (2011); Janowski and Rangel (2011); Laibson (1997).

[16] Nunes and Dreze (2006).

[17] This decision was not made a priori, but was determined based on the Paycheck Plus team's desire to have as many participants as possible attend a meeting and learn about how to earn the bonus in 2015.

[18] The factorial design enabled the BIAS team to test the effects of two manipulations at the same time (messaging type and delivery mode) on the dependent variable (meeting attendance). Using this design, the BIAS team explored the impact on meeting attendance for messaging type, for delivery mode, and for the two in combination. Thus, the study assessed the main effects of the two independent variables, as well as the interactions among them. In this case, a factorial design was more efficient than several simple randomized designs that tested one component against a control condition. However, when using the full sample in the factorial design to estimate the impact of the message type, the researcher is no longer estimating the average effect of only behavioral messaging compared with the standard messaging because half of the program group that received the behavioral message type also received the new delivery mode (postcards and texts). For a more detailed description of the tradeoffs, see Howard, Somers, and Taylor (2014).

[19] Appendix Figure A.1 shows how randomization was conducted.

[20] The subgroups' awareness of the EITC, earnings in the past year, and borough of primary residence are not presented because meaningful conclusions could not be drawn from the data. Distance to VITA sites is not presented because, upon further review, the BIAS team concluded that the way the variable was calculated — the distance between a participant's home address and the VITA site that was closest in mileage to that address — provided a measure that likely had little do to with whether a site was actually accessible to a participant. Within New York City's urban context, measuring distance "as the bird flies" often has little bearing on whether a location is accessible via public transportation, which is used universally. It is very possible that a VITA location farther away in mileage was easier to visit than one closer, if it was in close proximity to a convenient subway stop. Because no data were collected on which VITA site hosted the meeting that each participant attended, there is no way to know whether participants visited the location closest to their home address.

[21] Food Bank was only able to keep two of the original seven VITA sites open during Round 2 because the tax season was over by that time.

[22] The BIAS team also had concerns that in Round 1 multiple tenants could live in one household, and thus the materials might have been received by someone other than the intended recipient. In addition, the postcards could have been disregarded as part of the general marketing material that households receive.

[23] See Appendix Figure A.1 for how the sample was determined.

[24] The BIAS team assisted with preparing and sending certain forms of communication that were outside of Food Bank's capabilities (namely, personalized letters and personalized e-mails).

[25] Garner (2005).

[26] Sunstein (2003), Ross and Nisbett (1991); Service et al. (2014).

[27] Distribution lists were regularly updated to remove participants who attended a meeting.

[28] Participants who called the Food Bank hotline were usually told that they could also come in person and receive their gift card on the spot.

[29] There is evidence that these three elements of the Round 1 study improved the response rate. Implementation prompts were the central component of behavioral messaging, which was found to be more effective than standard messaging (Table 3); the conditions that included text messages in Round 1 generated a higher rate of response than those that included postcards alone (Table 3); and the incline of the survival plot lines suggests that as the deadlines approached, more people attended the meeting (Figure 4). This effect is more apparent in Figure 6, where it is verified with a log-rank test.

[30] Service et al. (2014).

[31] Touchette and Shapiro (2008); Lantz et al. (1995).

[32] In Round 2, only two offices were open for the informational meetings. They were located in Harlem and downtown Brooklyn, which are likely fairly accessible locations for most members of this sample. Because participants could only choose between two offices, they were not faced with the possible choice overload that members of the standard messaging groups may have confronted in Round 1.

[33] Kamenica (2012).

[34] See Ryan and Deci (2000) for a review of research on intrinsic motivation.

Suggested citation: Dechausay, Nadine, Caitlin Anzelone, Leigh Reardon (2015). *The Power of Prompts: Using Behavioral Insights to Encourage People to Participate*. OPRE Report 2015-75. Washington, DC: Office of Planning, Research and Evaluation, Administration for Children and Families, U.S. Department of Health and Human Services.

This report and other reports sponsored by the Office of Planning, Research and Evaluation are available at www.acf.hhs.gov/programs/opre.

INDEX

A

abuse, 30, 33
access, vii, 2, 3, 4, 5, 6, 9, 11, 13, 15, 16, 21, 26, 30, 36, 37, 40, 51, 53, 55, 106
adaptation, 12
Administration for Children and Families, 75, 77, 80, 83, 116, 118, 122
administrators, 77, 83, 86
adults, 77, 81, 99, 100, 120
advancement, vii, 114
age, 33, 73, 99
agencies, 2, 4, 5, 8, 10, 11, 12, 13, 14, 15, 16, 36, 37, 40, 41, 42, 58, 62, 68, 73, 120
appointments, 29
appropriations, 42
armed forces, 46
assets, 35, 61, 63, 64, 118
audit, 59
authority, 40, 42, 115
aversion, 55, 78, 90, 91, 92, 104, 114
awareness, 6, 23, 24, 26, 82, 99, 121

B

background information, 72, 73
barriers, vii, 3, 4, 6, 9, 14, 16, 25, 33, 53, 85
base, 5, 8, 14, 18, 19, 78, 106
basic research, 37
behavioral change, 4, 14, 103
behavioral sciences, vii, 1, 2, 4, 10, 11, 37, 40
behaviors, 30, 83
beneficiaries, 7, 11, 26, 29, 30, 41
benefits, 2, 4, 5, 6, 11, 12, 15, 16, 17, 18, 23, 24, 25, 29, 30, 36, 40, 41, 43, 44, 45, 52, 53, 54, 55, 73, 77, 82, 86, 92
bias, 90, 91, 92, 114, 115
bonds, 34
bonuses, 120
borrowers, 6, 11, 12, 21, 23, 24, 41, 50, 51, 52, 71
brain, 37
breakdown, 79
businesses, 11, 24, 30, 40

C

campaigns, 45, 56, 89
carbon, 9, 40
career counseling, 2, 4, 6, 11, 24, 36, 52, 53
causal inference, 14, 15
challenges, 12, 81, 82, 87, 88, 95, 107, 111
Chicago, 117
children, 37, 77, 81, 82, 119
chlorination, 29
cities, 49
clarity, 50
clients, 54, 83, 120
cognitive load, 91, 92

collaboration, 12, 23, 29, 37, 44, 45, 47, 50, 51, 53, 54, 55, 57, 58, 59, 66
collateral, 54
college students, 37
colleges, 6, 37, 120
color, 37
commercial, 26
communication, 53, 80, 103, 107, 114, 121
community(s), 2, 11, 37, 40, 68, 120
compensation, 18, 45
complexity, 70, 111, 115
compliance, 30, 33, 34
comprehension, 41
conference, 70, 72
consent, 80, 104, 115
Constitution, 40
consumers, 11, 41
consumption, 69
control condition, 121
control group, 49, 51, 82, 83
controlled substances, 7, 59
controlled trials, 85
conversations, 86, 100, 103
conversion rate, 8
cost, 1, 4, 6, 11, 13, 14, 15, 21, 23, 24, 29, 30, 33, 34, 35, 36, 37, 40, 42, 48, 49, 50, 52, 53, 57, 60, 66, 81, 83, 85, 104, 106
cost effectiveness, 11, 40
counseling, 53, 73
CPI, 59
credit history, 54
customers, 54, 60

D

danger, 50
data collection, 70, 72
deaths, 29
debts, 30, 31, 32, 58
decision makers, 30
deficit, 37
delinquency, 58
Department of Agriculture, 6, 13, 25, 66
Department of Defense, 5, 16, 43, 45, 47
Department of Education, 6, 21, 48, 50, 51, 69
Department of Health and Human Services, 7, 13, 26, 55, 74, 75, 77, 80, 116, 119, 122
Department of Labor, 13
Department of the Treasury, 7, 8, 32, 34, 58, 60
dependent variable, 121
designers, 114
detectable, 60
directives, 40
disclosure, vii, 3, 9
discomfort, 112
distribution, 106
doctors, 29
DOL, 13, 69
Domestic Policy Council, 37
drugs, 59

E

earnings, 21, 77, 81, 82, 99, 121
Economic Research Service (ERS), 8, 26, 36, 54, 66
economic well-being, 77
economics, 3, 9, 10, 30, 39, 69, 75, 77, 78, 81, 83, 84, 89, 120
education, 2, 4, 6, 11, 13, 21, 24, 36, 41, 52, 53
educational opportunities, 9, 40
electricity, 33
eligibility criteria, 23
e-mail, 80, 104, 106, 108, 121
employees, 5, 8, 13, 16, 18, 35, 36, 42, 43, 45, 46, 61, 62, 63, 64, 65, 66
employment, 24, 74, 77, 81-83, 99, 109, 120
employment opportunities, 24
employment status, 99
energy, 33
energy consumption, 33
enrollment, 3, 6, 7, 9, 10, 16, 17, 18, 19, 20, 21, 22, 25, 28, 36, 40, 43, 44, 45, 46, 47, 48, 49, 52, 55, 72, 82, 83, 86, 99

enrollment rates, 7, 19, 21, 43, 44, 46, 47, 48, 52
environment, 83
equity, 42
ERS, 8, 36, 66, 67
evidence, 1, 4, 9, 14, 15, 37, 39, 42, 59, 65, 121
executive branch, 66
Executive Order, 2, 9, 11, 37, 39, 41
experimental design, 81
expertise, 6, 21, 48, 72

F

families, vii, 2, 3, 4, 7, 9, 10, 11, 12, 13, 21, 26, 36, 40, 55, 77, 81, 82, 83
farmers, 6, 24, 25, 26, 36, 54, 55
farms, 2, 4, 11, 26, 36, 54
Federal Government, vii, 2, 3, 5, 8, 9, 10, 11, 12, 14, 16, 24, 26, 30, 31, 37, 40, 42, 43, 45, 64, 66
Federal Student Aid, 6, 21, 48, 50, 51
financial, vii, 2, 3, 9, 10, 12, 16, 17, 32, 33, 40, 45, 49, 56, 57, 81, 87, 99, 100, 112, 113
financial incentives, 113
fiscal year, 56
flu shot, 29
food, 13, 26, 69, 120
food safety, 26
framing, 17
fraud, 30, 33
funding, 56, 82

G

GAO, 74
General Services Administration (GSA), 7, 8, 10, 31, 32, 35, 57, 61, 63, 64
Georgia, 54
goods and services, 7, 31
governments, 69
guidance, 11, 37, 41, 42
guidelines, 115

H

health, vii, 2, 3, 4, 5, 7, 9, 11, 13, 16, 26, 28, 29, 33, 36, 55, 56, 59, 69, 87
health care, 13, 26, 28, 33
health insurance, vii, 2, 3, 4, 7, 9, 11, 26, 36, 55, 56
HHS, 7, 13, 26, 29, 37, 55, 69, 74
high school, 6, 21, 22, 37, 48, 50
HIV, 29
human, 29, 83
human behavior, 83
human immunodeficiency virus, 29

I

identification, 42, 61
image, 66
improvements, 2, 4, 8, 10, 11, 12, 13, 14, 29, 36, 40, 53
income, 1, 6, 13, 22-25, 37, 49, 50, 51, 72, 76, 77, 80, 81, 82, 86, 87, 111, 119, 120
income tax, 77, 81, 119
independent variable, 121
individuals, 7, 11, 12, 15, 17, 18, 26, 28-30, 32, 34-36, 40, 41, 50, 55, 58-60, 66, 67, 82, 83, 97, 98, 101, 108, 110, 111, 113
industry, 68
influenza, 29
influenza virus, 29
informed consent, 107
integrity, 2, 4, 7, 11, 12, 13, 30, 33, 34, 36, 59
interaction effect(s), 97
interface, 57
Internal Revenue Service, 119
intervention, 5, 15, 19, 22, 23, 32, 33, 67, 77, 78, 79, 81, 89, 90, 95, 100, 103, 109
intrinsic motivation, 122
investment(s), 4, 14, 25, 67, 83
investors, 34, 35, 60, 61
invitation to participate, 112
IRS, 70, 73, 116
issues, 77, 81, 83, 85, 103, 107

K

Kahneman, Daniel, 68-73, 83, 119
Kennedy, Kathleen, 118
Kenya, 29, 71

L

labeling, 12, 41
labor market, 13, 82
law enforcement, 33, 59
laws, 40
lead, 4, 9, 12, 35, 40, 53, 66, 72, 82
learning, 37, 81
legislative proposals, 42
lens, 75, 77, 81
light, 37, 80, 83, 104
loans, 2, 4, 11, 23, 25, 26, 36, 51, 54, 72
local government, 68
logistics, 46
Louisiana, 54
LTD, 34, 35, 60, 61, 74

M

magnitude, 107
majority, 95
management, 8
marital status, 119
marketing, 76, 80, 81, 89, 92, 94, 95, 98, 103, 104, 106-110, 112, 120, 121
marketing strategy, 92, 104
materials, 44, 62, 76, 80, 81, 90, 95, 98, 103, 107, 108, 112, 120, 121
matter, 8, 12, 14, 15, 30
media, 47
median, 31, 57
Medicaid, 7, 26, 33, 59, 83, 118
medical, 31, 59
Medicare, 7, 12, 26, 29, 32, 33, 59, 74
melt, 21, 22, 48, 49
memory, 88, 90, 114
mental energy, 113
mental health, 26
messages, 6, 17, 21, 22, 29, 35, 44, 45, 48, 49, 62, 63, 65, 76, 78, 79, 89, 94, 95, 97, 98, 99, 100, 101, 103, 106, 107, 108, 109, 110, 111, 121
methodology, 120
military, 5, 18, 20, 43, 45, 47, 52
missions, 4, 10
models, 83
modules, 96, 101, 109, 110
motivation, 92
Mozambique, 29
muscles, 37

N

National Academy of Sciences, 71-73, 118
negotiating, 113
neural connection, 37
neutral, 85, 91
nutrition, 69

O

Obama Administration, 1
Obama, President Barack, 9, 11, 24
obstacles, 100
Office of Management and Budget (OMB), 37, 42
officials, 7, 13, 30
Oklahoma, 113
operations, 2, 11, 26, 30, 34, 36, 40, 77, 81
opioids, 33, 59
opportunities, 2, 5, 11, 12, 16, 32, 37, 40, 41, 68, 84
organize, 99
outreach, 5, 8, 18, 26, 45, 52, 54, 76, 79, 80, 83, 89, 98, 99, 100, 103, 104, 108, 110, 111, 112, 113, 120
oversight, 74

P

pain, 114
parents, 37, 48, 49, 82, 83

participants, 12, 75, 76, 77, 78, 79, 80, 81, 82, 83, 84, 86, 87, 88, 89, 90, 91, 92, 95, 96, 98, 99, 100, 103, 104, 105, 106, 107, 108, 110, 111, 112, 115, 120, 121, 122
perseverance, 37
persuasion, 115
pharmaceuticals, 59
Philadelphia, 119
planned action, 114
platform, 8
pleasure, 114
policy, vii, 2, 3, 8, 10, 11, 12, 13, 14, 36, 37, 40, 41, 42, 46, 67, 68, 74
policy reform, 36
policymakers, 3, 9, 14, 15, 37
population, 48, 52, 54, 65, 82
portfolio, 4, 8, 13
potential benefits, 16, 44
poverty, 81, 82, 87, 113
precedents, 13
President, 2, 10, 11, 24, 37, 40, 41, 68
principles, 80, 85, 104
private sector, 16, 37
probability, 29
producers, 54
profit, 48
program administration, 4, 8, 10, 14, 15, 37
program outcomes, 2, 4, 11, 12, 13, 15, 40, 85, 120
project, 4, 12, 14, 18, 20, 21, 23, 26, 29, 32, 33, 34, 35, 36, 42, 48, 50, 66, 69, 72, 73, 75, 77, 80, 85, 113, 120
protection, vii, 3, 9
pruning, 37
psychologist, 83
psychology, 3, 9, 10, 39, 91
public domain, 122
public sector, 83
public welfare, 11, 40, 41

R

random assignment, 42, 46, 73, 98, 101, 107, 110, 111
reading, 103
reasoning, 99
recommendations, 12
recovery, 7, 58
reforms, 8, 14, 45
regression, 98, 101, 110, 111
regulations, 41
relevance, 12
remittances, 57
requirement(s), vii, 3, 5, 9, 42, 54, 77, 83
researchers, 6, 21, 37, 44, 48, 53, 59, 72, 86
resilience, 37
resistance, 30
resources, 12, 87, 92, 113, 114, 115
response, 8, 24, 35, 61, 62, 63, 65, 76, 79, 80, 92, 98, 99, 100, 103, 106, 107, 108, 112, 114, 121
retirement, vii, 1, 2, 3, 4, 5, 9, 10, 12, 13, 14, 16, 36, 40, 41, 45
rewards, 119
rights, 71
risk, 21, 24, 51, 52, 112
routines, 99
rules, 30, 83

S

savings, 1, 3, 5, 10, 14, 15, 16, 18, 21, 34, 36, 40, 43, 45, 46, 47
scaling, 5, 63, 65, 67
scarcity, 87, 90, 113
school, 9, 24, 37, 40, 49
science, vii, 1, 2, 3, 4, 9, 10, 11, 12, 15, 16, 18, 29, 30, 33, 35, 36, 37, 39, 40, 41, 60, 66, 67, 68, 77, 81, 83, 110
scientific method, 85
scope, 66, 83
security(s), vii, 3, 5, 8, 9, 13, 16, 34, 60
self-control, 83
self-interest, 84
self-reports, 56
self-sufficiency, 69
services, 24, 30, 35, 37, 53, 83
showing, 3, 10, 35, 58, 90, 91
significance level, 78, 79, 98, 101, 102, 110, 112

signs, 57
small business(s), 5, 16
social comparison, 58, 59
social influence, 104, 110
social network, 104
social programs, 110
Social Security, 16, 44, 47, 71, 73
social welfare, 2
society, 24, 26, 52
software, 67, 106
solution, 37
spending, 33, 34
state(s), 37, 54, 59, 63, 65, 68, 73, 83
statistics, 103
stress, 113
structure, 11, 12, 15, 41, 81
student achievement, 37
subgroups, 99, 102, 112, 121
survival, 95, 121

T

tangible benefits, 81
tax collection, 30, 58
tax incentive, vii, 3, 9
taxes, 12, 30, 41, 59, 77, 82, 104, 120
teams, 69
technical assistance, 70
techniques, 42, 76, 77, 80, 81
technology, 37, 67, 68
tenants, 63, 121
testing, 2, 56, 60, 64, 65
text messaging, 48, 50, 94
time periods, 5, 19
training, 24, 52, 120
traits, 37
transactions, 56
translation, 15
transportation, 121
Treasury, 34, 35, 43, 58, 60, 61
treatment, 29, 44, 46, 49, 51, 54, 57, 61, 66
trial, 53, 57, 58, 59
turnout, 100

U

U.S. Department of Agriculture (USDA), 6, 8, 13, 25, 26, 36, 54, 66, 69, 73
uniform, 73
uninsured, 55
United Kingdom, 58, 69
United States, 6, 25, 29, 40, 42, 71, 74, 75, 77, 81, 82
universities, 37
updating, 32
urban, 21, 48, 76, 80, 111, 121
Urban Institute, 37, 116, 118
urban population, 76, 80, 111

V

vaccinations, 29, 59
vocabulary, 37
vulnerable people, 75, 77, 81

W

wages, 77, 82
Washington, 116, 117, 118, 119, 122
waste, 30, 33
water, 29
web, 7, 23, 32, 33, 44, 54, 58
well-being, 77
White House, vii, 1, 3, 10, 18
workers, 3, 5, 9, 10, 16, 34, 40, 63, 82, 99, 100, 108
workforce, 16, 120
working groups, 68
workplace, 5, 8, 16, 18, 43, 45, 61, 63, 64, 65

Y

yield, 2, 4, 11, 14, 34, 40
young adults, 100